Śaṅkarāyaṇam

Advance Praise

'*Śaṅkarāyaṇam* is a well-written short biography of Śrī Ādi Śaṅkarācārya. The devotion of the author, Śrī Subramanian Chidambaran, is evident throughout as he presents the life journey of the great Ācārya. The work is short yet comprehensive, covering all pertinent aspects of the Ācārya's life. This insightful work gives attention to both facts and legends surrounding the life and work of the Ācārya, with references from some of the important *Śaṅkara-vijayas*. The author has also briefly covered the various important institutions established by the Ācārya and his prime disciples during their time, ensuring that the wisdom of Advaita-vedānta continues to reach us even millennia after the time of Śrī Ādi Śaṅkara. Congratulations to Śrī Subramanian Chidambaran for skilfully capturing the enduring legacy of Śrī Ādi Śaṅkarācārya in this engaging biography. I recommend this book to all those seeking to acquaint themselves with the glorious life of the Ācārya.'

Swami Advayananda
President, Chinmaya International Foundation

'Ācārya Śaṅkara is the greatest visionary, thinker, devotee, writer and a human being endowed with all virtues. We call such a person an incarnation of Isvara. This book will be an eye opener to see this Śaṅkara.'

Swami Sakshatkritananda Saraswati
Chairman and chief acharya, Swami Dayananda Ashram, Rishikesh

'Subramanian's book *Śaṅkarāyaṇam: The Journey of Śaṅkara* deserves to be read as a non-detailed text for any degree course in literature, culture, history and philosophy. His open-minded treatment of the much talked about date of Śaṅkara and the number of Śaṅkarācārya maṭhas, is highly commendable. The book will be of interest to the beginners as well as scholars on the subject.'

Dr Padma Subrahmanyam (Padma Vibhushan Awardee)
President, Nrithyodaya, Chennai

'This book, written by my good friend Subbu, will indeed be a very good contribution in generating the required awareness among people about the great Ācārya Ādi Śaṅkara, who strode this Bhāratavarṣa like a colossus and helped rejuvenate our Vedic Dharma.'

Dushyanth Sridhar
Vedic scholar and orator

Śaṅkarāyaṇam

The Journey of Śaṅkara

Subramanian Chidambaran

ink | OCCAM

ISBN: 978-93-6547-010-9

First published in India 2025
This edition published 2025

BluOne Ink Pvt. Ltd
A-76, 2nd Floor, Sector 136, Noida
Uttar Pradesh 201301
www.bluone.ink
publisher@bluone.ink

Printed and bound in India at Nutech Print Services

ink | OCCAM

ॐ नमो

ब्रह्मादिभ्यो

ब्रह्मविद्यासम्प्रदायकर्तृभ्यो

वंशऋषिभ्यो

नमो गुरुभ्यः

Contents

Foreword

Rāmāyaṇa is the journey of Rāma; on the same note, *Śaṅkarāyaṇam* is the journey of Ādi Śaṅkarācārya. Śaṅkara is one of the most prolific minds that Bhārat has ever produced. Ācārya was indeed a multifaceted personality of the highest order, and there is hardly any aspect of Sanātana-dharma that he did not influence. We have several biographies that have been written, and will be written, on such a popular personality. However, what I found different and refreshing in *Śaṅkarāyaṇam* by Subramanian (Subbu) Chidambaran, is that he has tried to create a seamless blend of storytelling and research while presenting the journey of the Ācārya. Subramanian Chidambaran, an ardent devotee of Ādi Śaṅkarācārya, has penned the journey with śraddhā and bhaktī, after listening to many discourses, and digesting the content of various books and monographs. Yet, this work is backed by a strong and unbiased research, at times even questioning the narratives that are popular amongst the masses, which lends it the required credibility.

The book is divided into eighteen chapters and, among others, provides a map of Ācārya's Digvijaya and an interesting FAQ section at the end. The most controversial topics in Ādi Śaṅkarācārya's life are the dates and places of his appearance and disappearance. The author has dealt with these issues in the end, with logical arguments and counterarguments, avoiding dry discussions. On the contrary, his storytelling technique makes the reading a delight and brings the story right in front of our eyes.

I am sure that this book, with its strong research backdrop, compelling storytelling, easy language and relatively compact size, will provide a literary, aesthetic, and above all, a devotional feast to readers of all categories. I wish Subbu all the best and may Ācārya keep showering his grace on him forever.

Dr Gauri Mahulikar
Academic Director,
Chinmaya International Foundation

Preface

Like most great personalities of yore in Bhāratavarṣa, we have a dearth of documentation on Ācārya's life as well, especially from his contemporaries or people who lived very close to his times. Most of the works on the Ācārya that we have today were written many centuries after his time. Until a century back, no one even knew where and when the Ācārya was born. Prostrations to the 33rd Jagadguru of Sringeri, H.H. Sacchidananda Shivabhinava Nrisimha Bharati Mahaswami, who rediscovered the birthplace of Ācārya as Kalady in Kerala and the day of birth as Vaiśākha-śukla-pañcamī, built a temple for the Ācārya there and called for Vaiśākha-śukla-pañcamī to be celebrated as Śaṅkara Jayanti! Hence, if we were to venture into analysing the life of the Ācārya historically, archaeologically, etc., and say with conviction on what happened and what did not, to me, that is a near impossible task!

What we have with us are the undisputed works of the Ācārya and the religious, temple and monastic traditions established by the Ācārya that have come down to us over generations, through oral traditions. Beyond these, we cannot do much, but have faith and devotion in our hearts, and pray to the Ācārya that he guides us to say what ought to be said. This has been the tradition of Bhārata. Do we not know the story of the Divya prabandhams being revealed to Nātha muni by Nammāzhvār through divine intervention, when they were physically lost to the world, and there was no 'practical, logical, historical' way of retrieving them back? Let the Ācārya, who is shining forth as the self within our hearts, himself write his story through us!

Hence, in all humility, I state that this work is no historical, archaeological or literary research on the Ācārya's life and work. While many of the extant biographies and works on the life of the Ācārya have been referred to in various places, this work is no comparative study or exhaustive review of them. It is a product of my intense desire to tell the story of the Ācārya as I see and experience in the light of Ācārya's works, the various discourses I have heard from great mahātmās, and what the Ācārya is making me say from within. I have, to the best of my efforts, tried to bring forth most of the relevant available information on the Ācārya in one place, so that it might help the jigñāsu – the ones who have an intense desire to know about the Ācārya.

I thank the Indic Academy, especially Dimple Kaul ji and Hari Kiran ji, who gave me an opportunity to present an online course on the life of the Ācārya (which triggered the idea to write this book), and now their support in publishing this book as part of the INDICA series with BluOne Ink. I thank Praveen ji and his team at BluOne Ink for their help in publishing this book. I thank Dimple Kaul ji, also for her continued support and guidance during the process of writing and publishing this book. I thank my guru and mentor, Professor Gauri Mahulikar, for her constant guidance and blessings, and also for agreeing to write the Foreword for this book. I thank Śrī Rama Seshan for going through the manuscript of this book and offering his valuable suggestions. I thank Swami Advayanand ji, Swami Sakshatkritanand ji, Dr Padma Subrahmanyam (Paddu akka), my friend Śrī Dushyanth Sridhar and Hari Kiran ji for blessing and providing their valuable suggestions and testimonials for this book.

I thank my parents, especially my mother, for introducing me to Śaṅkara. I thank my wife Kripa and son Shankar, for understanding and putting up with my schedules while writing this book. I thank my wife Kripa, also for diligently going through the script and providing her language edits. I thank everyone, who has, in some way or the other, sown the seed of Śaṅkara Bhakti in me.

My prostrations and eternal gratitude to the Ācārya, for choosing me as his instrument in this endeavour.

My Connection with Śaṅkara

The earliest memory I have of my association with the Ācārya is at the age of four, when I was dressed up as Śaṅkara by my mother, for my school fancy dress competition! As in many Tamizh Brāhmaṇa households, my day started with listening to the voice of M.S. Subbulakshmi Amma singing *Bhaja Govindam* of the Ācārya, the *Viṣṇu-sahasranāma* and 'Mudākarātta-modakam' (*Gaṇeśa-pañcaratnam* of Ācārya). Moreover, my mother, a musician herself, used to teach *Saundaryalaharī* (of Ācārya) and Mangadu Kāmākṣī Amman songs to many of her friends at home and I sat through most of these sessions. As a child, I would participate in numerous stotra competitions, for which I memorised several stotras written by the Ācārya. Though I did not understand the meaning of most at that young age, they were absorbed into my system unconsciously.

Being born and brought up in the locality of Matunga (Mumbai), which has a strong South Indian presence, we visited Shankara Matham every alternate day, or at least once a week. As a child, I was always enamoured by the marble statue of the Ācārya there, sitting in padmasana, that adorned the sanctum sanctorum. The life of the Ācārya, along with some of the prominent scholars in the Advaita-vedāntic tradition, was pictorially depicted across the walls of Shankara Matham, which held my attention as a child. I remember spending several minutes gazing at them. This was my first initiation into understanding the life of the Ācārya.

I vividly remember being among the most enthusiastic children to participate in all the kaiṅkaryam (services) to the Jagadgurus of Kanchi and Sringeri, when they visited my maternal native place in Thrissur, where I spent my annual summer vacations. Members of my maternal family have had strong associations with the Śaṅkara-maṭhas of Kanchi and Sringeri. Hence, I have heard, known and seen Śaṅkarācāryas pretty much all my life. I do have a faint memory, as a child of seven or eight years, having the darśana of my Guru, Kanchi Mahaswami (i.e., H.H. Śrī Chandrashekharendra Saraswati) who is revered as the 'walking God'. I have heard that, during one of His initial digvijayas (tours), when Mahaswami had camped in my ancestral village of Puthucode, my maternal great grandfather (fondly called 'Ambi'), who was the then panchayat president, had taught Malayalam to Mahaswami! It seems, whenever someone from our family went to meet Mahaswami, in later years, he would always ask 'How's Ambi?' One of my maternal grandfathers, Śrī M.R. Subramanian, was very closely associated with the Sringeri-maṭha, especially H.H. Śrī Abhinava Vidyatirtha Mahaswami and H.H. Śrī Bharati Tirtha Mahaswami. As a child, whenever I met him, he would narrate stories of his experiences, and the power of the Jagadgurus.

All these sowed the seed of bhakti in me, towards the Ācārya and the Śaṅkara paramparā. The seed slowly grew into a sapling, a plant and now, probably a tree!

During my days at IIM Lucknow, my devotion to the Ācārya, and understanding of Advaita-vedānta, was further enhanced by constantly listening to the lectures of Brahmasri Nochur Venkatraman (now known as Śrī Ramanacharana tirtha). I then got associated with the Sanskrit department at the University of Mumbai, where I did my M.A. in Sanskrit (with a specialisation in Vedānta). This brought me in touch with the Śāstric aspect of Ācārya's works, which only deepened by reverence, devotion and love towards the Ācārya, which has now taken the form of this book.

I strongly believe that it is the result of the good deeds done by me, my parents and my ancestors, in this or previous births, that Ācārya came into my life and has been continually growing inside me every moment!

गुरुपुङ्गव पुङ्गवकेतन ते समतामयतां नहि कोऽपि सुधीः ।
शरणागतवत्सल तत्त्वनिधे भव शङ्कर देशिक मे शरणम् ॥

O Best among the gurus! The Lord whose flag bears the emblem of the bull! You have no equal among the wise. You who are affectionate to those who seek refuge! The treasure of truth! O Preceptor Shankara, be my refuge. (Toṭakāṣṭakam verse 7)

ADHYĀYA 1

Prelude

यदा यदा हि धर्मस्य ग्लानिर्भवति भारत |
अभ्युत्थानमधर्मस्य तदात्मानं सृजाम्यहम् ||

O Bhārata! Whenever there is decay of
Dharma and the rise of Adharma,
I shall create myself (be born).

—Bhagavad Gītā 4.7

We, born in the land of Bhārata, belong to what is referred to as 'Sanātana-dharma', i.e., Eternal dharma. Dharma is a term that's been variedly defined and interpreted by scholars and others. Etymologically, that which sustains us is dharma.[1] Hence, dharma can be understood as the substratum on which our life – both as an individual and as a society is sustained. It's called eternal because there is no point in time, as far as we know, when it began. It's always been there. The basis of this Eternal dharma is knowledge. Another name for knowledge is Veda. Hence Vedas, which means a vast collection of knowledge, form the basis of this Eternal dharma.[2] Therefore, this dharma is also called Vedic dharma.

Now this Eternal dharma is twofold in nature– one that helps sustenance in this world – called pravṛtti-dharma and the other that helps us break out from the cycle of this world – nivṛtti-dharma and attain eternal sustenance.[3] When there is an immanent danger to this dharma, which endangers the sustenance of the individual and the society itself, then the Supreme Being manifests in a form, to uproot the source of danger and restore dharma. This is an assurance given by the Lord Himself in the Bhagavad Gītā.[4] This manifestation is what we refer to as an 'avatāra' or divine incarnation.

Sanātana-dharma has never been a uniform dharma, where everyone follows the same rites and rituals, believes in the same principles and worships the same powers. There has always been diversity of faiths, worships, rites, rituals, etc., within Sanātana-dharma, and this has always been encouraged. That is why, from time immemorial, in Sanātana-dharma, we find both believers and non-believers of God; we find people with varied worldviews living in harmony; and we find followers of cults practising tāmasic – such as occult rituals, animal sacrifices, rituals using meat, wine, sexual contact, etc., as well as sāttvic practices – everything accepted under Sanātana-dharma. The reason for this is that Sanātana-dharma recognises that all people are not the same and that everyone has a different inherent nature and disposition. This acceptance of diversity and providing that ecosystem is the uniqueness of Sanātana-dharma. However, when the aggressive and harmful aspects begin to overpower the society, problems begin to rise.

At such a juncture came Gautama Buddha, who, born into Sanātana-dharma, realised his true self–attained Nirvāṇa and took to the path of nivṛtti-dharma as enjoined in the Vedas. As far as the world was concerned, Buddha propagated a path of non-violence to bring balance in the society, which had probably become highly ritualistic and less concerned about understanding the relevance and essence behind the rituals.

Attracted by Buddha's aura, many took to his followership and became 'bhikkus' or bhikṣus. Though saṁnyāsa and bhikṣā as a means of life has always been there in Sanātana-dharma, it was an individual choice and never an organised affair. It was probably for the first time, during the time of Buddha and later, that the world saw an organised set of saṁnyāsīs with organised institutions and royalty backing them. Over a period, the teachings and the way of life of the Buddha suffered serious interpolations and misunderstandings, and people began abandoning the Vedic way of life – primarily the enjoined actions and joining the bhikṣu system, to lead an easy and convenient life. This posed a danger to the sustenance of Sanātana-dharma, which necessitated the advent of a divine manifestation. This is the background to the birth of Śaṅkara.

It may be noted here that even when the later proponents of Sanātana-dharma heavily criticised Buddhism and Jainism, they never had the least disrespect for the Buddha or Mahāvīra. The criticism was hurled at the degraded system of followership that was prevalent in those times. Swami Vivekananda, in his lectures, says that the real essence of Buddhism and Vedānta are not very different and that the disciples of Buddha did not understand the Master, and thus have degraded themselves. While Buddha stressed upon the moral side of Vedānta, Śaṅkara emphasised the intellectual and experiential side.

The coming of Buddhism, and later Jainism, was probably the first formation of sects, or what we refer to as 'religions' today, outside of Sanātana-dharma. Though, technically, the tenets of these sects are drawn very much from Sanātana-dharma itself, they preferred to keep themselves separate from their parent, i.e., Sanātana-dharma. This later paved the way for formation of Semitic religions – Judaism, Christianity and Islam and other religions of the world. All this necessitated Sanātana-dharma to be referred to as a religion. It was given the name 'Hinduism'. The term 'Hindu' appears nowhere in the Vedic literature. This was a term given by the Persians to the civilisation that flourished on the banks of the river Sindhu – the Indus valley civilisation. The syllable 'Sa' became 'Ha' in their language and thus 'Sindhu' became 'Hindu' and 'Saindhava-dharma' became 'Haindava-dharma'.[5]

ADHYĀYA 2

The Divine Descent

अज्ञानान्तर्गहनपतितान् आत्मविद्योपदेशैः त्रातुं लोकान्
भवदवशिखातापपापच्यमानान् |
मुक्त्वा मौनं वटविटपिनोः मूलतो निष्पतन्ति शम्भोर्मूर्तिश्चरति भुवने
शङ्कराचार्यरूपा ||

To protect the people who have fallen into the deep recess of ignorance and are being cooked in the heart of the fire of the world, Śambhu forewent his silence, left his abode under the banyan tree, descended onto this world and is walking as Śaṅkarācārya.

—*Madhavīya-śaṅkara-vijaya* 4.60

It is a commonly accepted view that Ācārya was born into a Nambūdiri family in the village of Kalady in modern-day Kerala, several centuries ago. What we know as Kerala today was earlier referred to as 'Mala-nāḍu' – or the hilly region and was part of the ancient Tamizhakam, i.e., Tamizh land. Purāṇas state that the linear piece of land stretching from Gokarna in the north to Kanyakumari in the south (that includes, in the modern context, the state of Kerala and parts of coastal Karnataka) is referred to as

'Paraśurāma-kṣetra', as this piece of land is said to have been reclaimed by Lord Paraśurāma by throwing his axe into the ocean. This is probably one of the earliest examples of sea–land reclamation! Paraśurāma is then said to have divided this landmass into sixty-four parts and brought in sixty-four Brāhmaṇa families from different parts of Bhārata to inhabit these. These Brāhmaṇas came to be called the 'Nambūdiri' Brāhmaṇas, and this is commonly understood as the origin of the Nambūdiri community in Kerala. Many traditional scholars believe that these Brāhmaṇas came into Kerala, from the banks of the rivers Narmada, Krishna and Kaveri. Kanchi Mahaswami says that many of these Brāhmaṇas must have come from the Andhra and Karnataka regions because the house of Nambūdiris is called 'illam' or 'mana',[1] both of which are words for a house in Telugu (illu) and Kannada (mane) respectively.

The origin of the name 'Nambūdiri' is unknown. The term 'nambi' – literally means one who can be depended upon, is a common term in Tamizh culture. In fact, nambi is one of the names by which the Āzhvārs refer to Lord Nārāyaṇa Himself![2] Some opine that Nambūdiri is an evolution of the terms 'nambi' and 'ādari' – trust and respect, which essentially refers to people who can be trusted and respected, i.e., the 'āptas'. Some give the etymology as '*nam (Vedam) pūrayati iti*', i.e., one who completes the Vedas (Vedic studies and its practice).

It is believed that Lord Varāha was the iṣṭa-devata – favourite deity of these Brāhmaṇa families that settled in Paraśurāma-kṣetra, and hence the first temple consecrated by Paraśurāma in Kerala was that of Varāha in Panniyur in the Palakkad district of Kerala. The temple is believed to be four thousand years old, which might also be the time when the Nambūdiri Brāhmaṇas settled in this region.

When we look at the deity-worship in Kerala, we primarily see worship of Śiva in various forms, especially as Liṅga and Kirāta, Durgā – more commonly called Bhagavatī, Viṣṇu in various forms, Śāstā and Nāga. We would find Gaṇapati mostly as a parivāra devata – subsidiary deity. In most of these temples, worship is done by the Nambūdiris; they have always been a community worshipping many deities in harmony. Hence, this came very naturally to the Ācārya, who, in his later years, went on to establish the six theistic traditions of worship as well as propagate oneness amongst all deities.

Both the paternal and maternal lineages of Ācārya were Nambūdiri Brāhmaṇas. The paternal grandfather of Ācārya was one Vidyādhirājā or Vidyādhara as per the Śaṅkara-vijayas. Nothing much is known about Vidyādhirājā except that he settled in the village of Kalady. His son was Śivaguru, the father of our Ācārya. Śivaguru is said to have been a kulapati (a principal in the modern context) of Vedic gurukulas. Scholar T.M.P. Mahadevan states that Śivaguru is a unique name not found very commonly amongst Nambūdiri Brāhmaṇas, except if it was the name of their family deity or the deity of the place the family hailed from.[3] Now, the only temple with the presiding deity as Śivaguru is the Śivagurunāthasvāmi temple in Shivapuram near Kumbhakonam in Tamil Nadu. Hence, Mahadevan suggests that the ancestors of the Ācārya would have migrated from Shivapuram. They probably first settled in the current region of Thrissur and in remembrance of their ancestral village, they gave the name to the new place as 'Tiru-Śiva-puram'. 'Puram' or place would translate in Tamizh as 'ūr'. Hence, the name became 'Tiru-Śiva-per (name)-ūr' or Thrissur in later days. They probably would have shifted to Kalady later. It is believed that Śivaguru's ancestral home in Kalady was called the Kaippiḷḷi mana.

As regards the maternal ancestry of the Ācārya, we understand that his mother was the daughter of one Magha (or Makha) paṇḍita, belonging to the Melpāzhūr mana in modern-day Ernakulam. Though we commonly refer to Ācārya's mother as Āryāmbā, only the works of Cidvilāsa and Brahmānanda Sarasvati mention it so. Madhavīya-śaṅkara-vijaya (MSV) and Śaṅkara-abhyudaya (SA) do not mention her name at all. Bhagavatpāda-abhyudaya (BA) mentions the name as Satī, while Śaṅkara-abhyudaya-kāvya (SAK) mentions it as Vimalā. BA further says that, because she was so noble and a woman of great qualities like Goddess Umā, she was called 'Āryā' and 'Ambā'! We will henceforth refer to the mother as Āryāmbā, as she was the mother of Ācārya – the noblest person or Ārya, that Bhārata has ever produced.

Advaita-Rājya-lakṣmī ṭīkā and *ḍiṇḍima-ṭīkā* on MSV state that Śivaguru belonged to the *Taittirīya-śākhā* of *Yajurveda* since this branch was the dominant branch in Kerala then.[4] They also mention that while commenting on the first *Brahma-sūtra* 'athāto brahma jigñyāsā', Ācārya quotes mainly from *Taittirīya-upaniṣad* and not from other Upaniṣads that have similar statements. In earlier days, it was a practice for Vedic scholars to start any work on the Vedas with the branch of Veda they belonged to.[5] Hence in keeping up with this tradition, it is believed that Ācārya belonged to the *Kṛṣṇa-yajurveda*. Swami Chinmayananda (1978) and Swami Mukhyananda (2006) of Ramakrishna Mission also concur to the same.

It is worth noting that even today, we get to see some of the Vedic rituals, such as atirātram and somayāga, in practice only among the Nambūdiri community in Kerala. Hence, before Ācārya's birth, the Vedic ecosystem should have been even more vibrant and widespread in Kerala.

Śivaguru and Āryāmbā kept performing the duties prescribed for householders with all dedication and devotion. As years rolled by and they attained middle age, they became concerned with the absence of any progeny. It may be noted here that Vedas mention progeny as an essential aspect of the life of a gṛhastha primarily from the perspective of having an heir to take ahead the Vedic tradition. Swami Vivekananda, in his lecture delivered at California, says, 'your children, if they come without prayer, will prove a curse to humanity'.[6] This has been the tradition of Sanātana-dharma. Parents must yearn for progeny and perform penance towards the same. Stronger the penance, nobler is the child born. Wasn't that how Lord Rāma and Lord Kṛṣṇa were born? Hence, the delay in the advent of Śaṅkara was the time needed for Śivaguru and Āryāmbā to become the right recipients, both emotionally and spiritually, of this divine being! Connected with this is an interesting back-story. It is said that even during his childhood, Śivaguru was extremely drawn to renouncing the world and seeking self-realisation. Hence, he did not wish to marry after the completion of his education. However, his father strongly objected to this and requested the teacher to advise Śivaguru to agree for marriage. The teacher then mentioned to Śivaguru that Lord Śiva Himself would be born as his son, and it is only apt that he goes back home and agrees for the marriage. The authenticity of the story aside, it proves useful in ascertaining the qualification for Śivaguru, with such high levels of dispassion, to be the father of Śaṅkara! One is reminded here of the story of the father of Sant Jñāneśvar, who, after marriage, took to renunciation, leaving his wife behind because of the extreme dispassion he had. Then, at the behest of his guru, he came back to his wife and gave birth to four children – Nivṛttināth, Jñāneśvar, Sopāndev and Muktābāi – each one of whom became Self-realised beings!

Āryāmbā recommended Śivaguru to intensify their worship to the Lord. As advised by the elders, the couple undertook 'bhajana' for a period of one maṇḍala, i.e., 48 days, at the temple of Vṛśabhācala in Thrissur. Bhajana is a ritual where an individual spends the whole day in the temple, witnesses all the pūjās, partakes of the nivedya offered and sleeps the night in the premises itself. It may be noted here that Thrissur, with temple of Vṛśabhācala at its centre, was a hub of Vedic learning in those days, and it was a practice for the Nambūdiri brahmacārīs to spend a year at the temple in bhajana after their completion of education. Hence, the practice of doing bhajana at the Vṛśabhācala temple was well known to both Śivaguru and Āryāmbā.

The Śiva-liṅga at Vṛśabhācala is said to have self-manifested prior to the advent of Śaṅkara,[7] as though to indicate the arrival of Śiva in a human form as Śaṅkara! This is the temple of Vṛśabhācala (literally the 'hill of the bull') translated into Tamizh as Viḍava-kuṇḍru. Hence, the Lord here came to be called Vṛśabhācaleśvara or Viḍava-kuṇḍru-nāthan, which later got transformed as Vadakkunnathan! This temple holds a special position for the Nambūdiri communities of Kerala. Every young Nambūdiri belonging to *Ṛgveda*, having completed his upanayana, had to undergo one year of bhajana at the Vadakkunnathan temple. Those belonging to *Yajurveda* had to undergo the same at the Taliparamba Rājarājeśvara temple in modern-day Kannur district of Kerala.

As a result of the intense devotion of Śivaguru and Āryāmbā, the Lord blessed the couple in their dreams that He Himself would be born as their son. Extremely happy and satisfied with this divine experience, the couple came back to Kalady. Soon, Āryāmbā showed signs of pregnancy. One day, she felt a divine light entering her womb! On the fifth day of the bright fortnight of the month of Vaiśākha, was born the divine child Śaṅkara who, true to his name, was to do the greatest good to mankind![8] It is interesting to note that none of the older works on the Ācārya such as the MSV, Prācīna Śaṅkara Vijaya (PSV) or Bṛhat Śaṅkara Vijaya (BSV) mention of the date of birth of the Ācārya. Naming of a child is one of the important Vedic samskāras (called Nāmakaraṇa) performed on different days after birth, as per different traditions. The Gṛhya sutras lay down various rules for naming the child.[9]

Sanātana-dharma speaks of 16 major events in the life of a person. These are called 'saṁskāras'. The purpose of these saṁskāras, true to the meaning, is to help 'refine' the individual mentally and spiritually. It starts with 'garbhādhāna', i.e., placing the seed of the father in the womb of the mother and ends with 'antyeṣṭī', i.e., the funeral rites. Thus, the saṁskāras and through them, the Vedic mantras, govern the entire life of the follower of Sanātana-dharma.

Among the various customs followed in olden days, one was to name the child using a numerical formula that indicated the birthday of the child. The formula worked thus - the first alphabet signified the tithi (the day of the fortnight) of birth, second alphabet signified the pakṣa (the fortnight) and third alphabet signified the month (as per Hindu calendar). Numbers are then assigned to the alphabets using various methods, of which kaṭapayādi is one method. In this, the Sanskrit alphabet series beginning with *ka*, *ṭa*, *pa*, and *ya* are given numbers starting from one to nine and ten is represented as zero. According to this, *śa* is fifth in the *ya*-series, *ka* is first in the *ka*-series and *ra* is second in the *ya*-series. Thus, Śaṅkara represents the numbers five–one–two, i.e., fifth tithi (pañcamī), first pakṣa (śukla) and second month (vaiśākha), which translates to vaiśākha-śukla-pañcamī! This is what is celebrated as Śaṅkara Jayanti even to this day. This is corroborated by BA, which states that Śaṅkara was born as an amśa of Rudra in madhu-māsa (another name for vaiśākha), sita (śukla) pakṣa and in pañcamī tithi. It additionally mentions the nakṣatra (star) as that of Rudra (i.e., ārdrā).[10] Another version states that Śivaguru was chanting the *Rudra-praśna* and the news of the birth of the child reached him when he was chanting the mantra from the eighth anuvāka (paragraph) '*Namaḥ Śaṅkarāya ca*'. He, hence, named the child Śaṅkara.

ADHYĀYA 3

The Making of the Mumukṣu

दुर्लभं त्रयमेवैतद्देवानुग्रहहेतुकं मनुष्यत्वं मुमुक्षुत्वं महापुरुषसंश्रयः ।

Human birth, longing for liberation and the protecting care of a perfected sage are three things that are indeed rare and come by the grace of God.

—*Viveka-cūḍāmaṇi* verse 3

Śaṅkara was born in an environment that resounded with Veda mantras all day, especially given that Śivaguru was a kulapati of the Vedic schools in the vicinity. Hence, much of the Vedic study must have gotten absorbed into Śaṅkara by just being in that environment. In most probability, Malayālam as a language did not exist during the time of Śaṅkara. The spoken language must have been Tamizh and Sanskrit. Many scholars believe that Malayālam is a language that emerged later, as a combination of Tamizh and Sanskrit.

Śivaguru passed away when Śaṅkara was just three years old. This must have indeed been a difficult time for both Āryāmbā and Śaṅkara. In the ancient days, in the event of death of the husband, it was customary for the wife, along with her children, to start staying at her maternal home. However, Āryāmbā did not do so, and continued to stay in Kalady. The relatives on either side, as well as well wishers of Śivaguru would have helped Āryāmbā run the family. We also understand that Śivaguru was a priest at the nearby temple of Goddess Kātyāyanī. Their family deity was Lord Kṛṣṇa, whose temple was next to Śivaguru's house. Āryāmbā used to regularly take bath in the river and visit these temples as a daily ritual. Hence, it is possible that Āryāmbā did not want to go away from this ambience that she was accustomed to for so many years.

Śaṅkara continued to grow under the love and discipline of his mother and surrounded by the serene atmosphere of temples, rivers and Vedic rituals. It is very much possible that Āryāmbā taught him many verses and stories from the Itihāsas and Purāṇas. While feeding him food that nourished his body, she also infused into him adherence to our Vedic dharma and devotion to the Lord, which nourished his soul. As the Upaniṣads say, the child who is well taught by the mother first and later by the father and the guru, becomes eligible for the knowledge of Brahman.[1] Here, Āryāmbā was both the mother and father to Śaṅkara! This sowed the seeds of greatness in Śaṅkara, which would later manifest itself in the most splendorous form, providing refuge and solace to the world! As a child, Śaṅkara was indeed a prodigy. He could grasp things by hearing or reading once (eka-santha-grāhī).

Śaṅkara was now five years old. It was time for the next important saṁskāra in his life – the upanayana (investing of the sacred thread). Śāstras prescribe eight years (from the time of the foetus development) as the age for upanayana for Brāhmaṇas. However, in exceptional cases, based on the child's maturity, it prescribes the age of five as well. Considering this, and noting the immense maturity and intellect of Śaṅkara, Āryāmbā wanted to have the upanayana performed at the age of five. Some opine that the upanayana was performed by the maternal family of Śaṅkara in the Melpāzhūr mana (the Chinmaya International Foundation has currently set up their campus surrounding this).

Upanayana, literally, provides an additional (upa) pair of eyes (nayana), i.e., a divine insight, which is developed in the child by the constant chanting of the 'sāvitrī' (gayatri) mantra. This is the key to unlocking the knowledge and wisdom of the Vedas, which then leads the child to the ultimate truth of the Upaniṣads leading to liberation! Hence, after the upanayana, Śaṅkara was enrolled in a gurukula to commence his Vedic studies. It is said that within a span of two–three years, Śaṅkara completed his education having mastered the aṣṭādaśa-vidyā-sthānas (eighteen seats/ branches of knowledge) taught in Vedic schools in ancient times.[2] Śaṅkara must have also mastered the various darśana-śāstras (schools of philosophy), culminating in the study of the Upaniṣads. For a prodigious child like Śaṅkara, who grew up in an atmosphere resounding with these subjects all day, this came as no surprise. As was the practice in gurukulas, the students had to go to the households in the vicinity for bhikṣā every day and gather food, which was to be handed over to the guru and his wife for cooking and feeding all the students. Also, the society was such that the householders yearned for the merit of offering bhikṣā to the brahmacārīs. During one such bhikṣa, Śaṅkara reached the door of a Brāhmaṇa who was living up to the ideals enjoined in the śāstras that prohibit a Brāhmaṇa from hoarding anything including food, even for one day! The Brāhmaṇa was not at home and his wife came out of the house hearing a young brahmacārī calling out '*bhavati bhikṣām dehi*' – O Mother! Give me some food. The spiritual aura of the young Śaṅkara captivated her. Her heart wanted to give a bountiful bhikṣā to the brahmacārī, but she had nothing at home to offer except for an old, dried gooseberry. This wrenched her heart. With great sorrow, she offered that gooseberry to Śaṅkara as bhikṣā, feeling extremely guilty that she could not give anymore. Vedas say that one must give charity matching one's ability, opulently with humility and fear of not generating pride in oneself by this act.[3] The bhikṣā of the Brāhmaṇa lady exemplified this. Touched by this act of generosity and feeling happy and overwhelmed by the life the Brāhmaṇa and his wife were leading in strict adherence to the Vedas, Śaṅkara spontaneously uttered a set of verses appealing to Śṛī, the Goddess of wealth and prosperity, to shower her bounteous blessings on the Brāhmaṇa and his wife. It is said that on the completion of the verses, there rained a shower of golden gooseberries on that modest Brāhmaṇa home. These verses are popularly known as *Kanakadhāra* (shower of gold)-*stava*. In later days, the house of this Brāhmaṇa came to be called the 'Svarṇathu mana' (the golden house). This house and the descendants of that Brāhmaṇa are there even today, near Kalady. They say that even during the times of famine and drought, the family remained largely unaffected and had enough wealth for a comfortable living. This they believe is because of the blessings of the Ācārya on their ancestor! As one reads the *Kanakadhāra-stava*, it is impossible to imagine that such a masterpiece of poetry would have come from a five- or six-year-old child. The blessed land of Bhārata is full of such anecdotes. Didn't a three-year-old child (Tiru-jñāna-sambandar) in Sirkazhi sing 'Toḍuḍaiya Seviyan'? Logic has little role to play in Divinity!

Having completed his studies, Śaṅkara firmly concluded that the Ultimate truth is that which is espoused in the Upaniṣads, and to realise that (i.e., realise one's true nature as Brahman) is the sole aim of human life. Having returned home after completion of studies, Śaṅkara spent nearly a year, contemplating on the message of the Upaniṣads and doing ātma-vicāra (self-enquiry). Having understood the futility of worldly life, the desire for liberation grew intensely within the young mumukṣu (the one desirous of liberation).

During this time, the fame of Śaṅkara as a prodigy reached the ears of the king of Kerala who visited Śaṅkara and offered gifts. Śaṅkara respectfully rejected them stating that it would be better utilised if distributed amongst the needy, and that the Lord is there to take care of the needs of his mother and him – such was the faith in that young brahmacārī towards the Lord. Here, we are reminded of the assurance Kṛṣṇa gives in the *Gītā*, that he takes care of all the physical and spiritual needs of a person who is undividedly devoted to Him.[4] Before taking leave, the king shared three of his dramas with Śaṅkara and solicited his inputs on them.

This king is named as Rājaśekhara in many versions. He must have been one of the Cera kings who ruled the region of Thrissụr/Cochin during that time. 'Indian Archaeology 2010–11: A Review' mentions of a 9th-century inscription that mentions of a king Rājaśekhara who belonged to the Ikṣvāku dynasty and ruled the land justly like Manu. We do not find any extant dramas attributed to any Rājaśekhara of Kerala. The earliest Sanskrit dramas in Kerala (Subhadrā-dhanañjaya and Tapatī-saṁvaraṇa) are those of one Kulaśekhara Varman who is said to have introduced the art form of Kūḍiyāṭṭam, the earliest indigenous theatre of Kerala, to stage these dramas and thus revived Sanskrit dramas in Kerala. We don't know if the same Kulaśekhara is referred to as Rājaśekhara here.

Somewhere deep in her heart, Āryāmbā knew that Śaṅkara was not made for the worldly life of a householder. She, however, resisted this thought, given her unconditional love for Śaṅkara, and the fact that he was her only support in life. Śaṅkara also loved his mother dearly. He, through his yogic powers, had turned the course of the river (where Āryāmbā went daily to take bath) to flow through the backyard of his house, so that his mother did not have to walk a long distance to take bath. The river, which is called Periyar today, is mentioned in different versions as Pūrṇā or Cūrṇā. With the new course of the river, it is said that the temple walls of the Kṛṣṇa temple nearby were getting eroded, and hence Śaṅkara reconsecrated the vigraha of Kṛṣṇa in a nearby place. This Kṛṣṇa temple can be seen even today next to the Sringeri-maṭha in Kalady. Ācārya is said to have composed the *Kṛṣṇāṣṭakam* in praise of his family deity in Kalady. This was the first consecration of a vigraha done by the Ācārya, which was to be followed by many more in years to come.

Consecration of a vigraha is no simple activity in Sanātana-dharma. It involves various rites and rituals. The concept is of infusing life into a vigraha made of stone or wood or metal or other material. This, as per the Kerala-tantric tradition, is done by a Tantrī who draws energy from his own self and infuses it into the vigraha making it a 'living entity'. The Tantrī, is hence, regarded the father of the deity. Śaṅkara, coming from a Nambūdiri community, probably had great understanding of the antric rituals required for the consecration and worship in temples. This is amply reflected in the later life of the Ācārya.

As if to validate Āryāmbā's concerns, there appeared on the scene a few Brāhmaṇas, who, in the guise of taking bhikṣā, communicated two messages. They said to Āryāmbā, 'O blessed Mother, your son is a divine child born to resurrect the declining Sanātana-dharma and not lead the life of a householder. Hence, you must allow him to go behind this bigger cause.' Then they looked at the young Śaṅkara standing beside his mother – they could see a soul that was desperately looking for a guru who could assuage its burning desire for liberation by showing the right path. They told Śaṅkara. 'O blessed child, the only one who can show you the right path leading to the Ultimate truth is Govinda Bhagavatpāda, the disciple of the great Gauḍapāda. He is residing on the banks of the Narmada, in the sacred land of Omkareshwar. He is eagerly waiting for you.' These words from the Brāhmaṇas felt, to Śaṅkara, like heavy showers of rain pouring down on a land parched for water!

Now Śaṅkara, all of eight years of age, was determined and intent on undertaking the journey to his guru. Though the thought of leaving his mother saddened him and he did not want to disappoint her, the burning desire for liberation inside him was far more to be obstructed by these feelings. Then, as if divinely staged, an incident took place. One day, as Śaṅkara went to take bath in the river, a crocodile caught his leg. The pain was unbearable, and the crocodile was pulling Śaṅkara into the waters. A helpless Āryāmbā, who was standing on the banks, shouted and cried profusely seeing her son getting drowned and being devoured by the crocodile. She could see the end of her dear son coming closer; she could do nothing but pray to the Lord for some miracle to happen. Śaṅkara too knew that his end was near. As was the custom, Śaṅkara requested Āryāmbā to give him permission for āpat-saṁnyāsa, i.e., taking saṁnyāsa at a moment of peril when the moment of death is near. Reluctantly, Āryāmbā gave the permission. The moment Āryāmbā gave her approval, the crocodile mysteriously left Śaṅkara and disappeared into the waters! Āryāmbā understood that this was part of a divine play and she just had to stand by the divine will. With a heavy heart, but for the greater good of the world, that great mother bid farewell to her only son whom she loved so dearly. Śaṅkara, however, assured her that he would be by her side when she needed him the most. Prostrations to the sacrifice of that mother!

ADHYĀYA 4

The Union of Guru and Śiṣya

तद्विज्ञानार्थं स गुरुमेवाभिगच्छेत्समित्पाणिः श्रोत्रियं ब्रह्मनिष्ठम् |

To acquire the knowledge of the eternal, one should approach a realised being well versed in the Vedas and centred in the Brahman with the sacrificial fuel in hand.

—*Muṇḍaka-upaniṣad* 1.2.12

तद्विद्धि प्रणिपातेन परिप्रश्नेन सेवया |
उपदेक्ष्यन्ति ते ज्ञानं ज्ञानिनस्तत्त्वदर्शिनः ||

Learn the truth by approaching a spiritual master. Inquire from him with reverence and render service unto him. Such an enlightened being can impart knowledge unto you because he has seen the truth.

—Bhagavad Gītā 4.34

The young eight-year-old brahmacārī began his journey towards his guru. The journey from central Kerala, down south, to Madhya Pradesh in the central part of the country, even today, is replete with risks, given the landscape of dense forests inhabited by wild animals and many large rivers that one needs to cross. Imagine undertaking this journey several centuries ago, and that too on foot! It would have taken months for Śaṅkara to undertake this journey across dense forests of modern-day Kerala, Karnataka, Maharashtra and Madhya Pradesh as well as crossing rivers Bharatapuzha, Kaveri, Tunga, Krishna, Godavari and Tapi before reaching the banks of the river Narmada! What kept this child going? Indeed, the burning desire for liberation and knowing the Supreme truth!

Śaṅkara probably would have taken the help of peripatetic traders who knew the lay of the land and could provide guidance through the journey. Also, the journey would have been along riverbanks, as in those days, rivers provided for all the water needed for sustenance as well as daily rituals. Walking several miles, he reached the banks of the river Tunga in Karnataka, where he witnessed an unnatural scene. A huge cobra was protecting a pregnant frog from the scorching heat of the sun by spreading its hood over it. How is the cobra protecting the frog that is its natural prey? Śaṅkara understood that this was no ordinary place. He remembered the verse from the Yoga-sūtra, which says that in the presence of the one who is established in non-violence, even natural enmity is forgotten![1] On enquiry from the local elders, he understood that this was the place where centuries ago Ṛṣis Ṛṣyaṣṛṅga and his father Vibhāṅḍaka had performed penance and finally merged into the Divine. The place was hence called Ṛṣyaṣṛṅga-giri which later got renamed into Sringeri. The Śiva-liṅga worshipped by Vibhāṅḍaka, into which he finally merged, is today referred to as Malahānikareśvara, and is situated atop a hill close to the Sringeri-maṭha. The Śiva-liṅga worshipped by Ṛṣyaṣṛṅga is in a place called Kigga close to Sringeri. The Jagadgurus of Sringeri-maṭha, until today, regularly visit these two temples and pay their respects. This place remained etched in Śaṅkara's heart.

In another version, Śaṅkara is said to have left Kalady along with his childhood friend Viṣṇu, who he lost while crossing one of the major rivers en route Omkareshwar. This childhood friend of Ācārya later met him in Kashi and became his disciple assuming the name Citsukha.

After many more days of travel, Śaṅkara reached the banks of Narmada. This was the first journey of Śaṅkara outside his birthplace that exposed him to the various cultures and religious traditions of Bhārata, which is reflected in the later events of Śaṅkara's life.

On reaching the banks of Narmada, Śaṅkara enquired about Govinda Bhagavatpāda. He was directed to a group of caves on the Māndhāta Island on Narmada. This is the place where Ṛṣi Māndhāta is said to have performed penance. In those days, saṁnyāsīs chose to stay in caves, as is evident from the Buddhist vihāras. These caves were natural locations that provided coolness and water during summer and protected against the cold and rains during the other seasons. Govinda Bhagavatpāda, being one of the foremost and probably the only guru of Advaita-vedānta during his time, had many disciples. Hence, Śaṅkara was easily guided by them to the cave where Govinda Bhagavatpāda was in meditation. The very presence of Śaṅkara generated waves of inexplicable happiness in the calm mind of the guru. He opened his eyes and beheld the young Śaṅkara standing in front of him, beaming with the brilliance of knowledge, dispassion and an intense desire for liberation. The guru asked Śaṅkara, 'Who are you child?' In response to this question, Śaṅkara uttered a set of ten verses (popularly called *Daśaślokī*), which started as 'I am not the earth or water or fire or air or space or the senses or their combination. I am the one who is evident in deep sleep. I am the One, the residual, the most auspicious One. That alone I am.'[2] A doubt could arise here. The ten verses seem to clearly indicate the experience of the Ultimate non-dual Brahman. If Śaṅkara was already realised, as is evident from the verses, why did he have to travel all the way in search of the guru? It might be prudent to say that though the desire for liberation in Śaṅkara was most intense, the realisation of the non-dual Self dawned in the presence of Guru Govinda Bhagavatpāda, by His grace. Śaṅkara says in the *Viveka-cūḍāmaṇi* that even with all the desired qualities in a student, it is in the presence of the guru that the knowledge truly bears fruit.[3] We could also say that this is how Śaṅkara set an example for the world, like Rāma and Kṛṣṇa, that the grace of the guru is a critical aspect in realisation of the Supreme. This was the birth of Śaṅkara – the jīvanmukta!

As per the tradition, Govinda Bhagavatpāda formally initiated Śaṅkara into saṁnyāsa and gave him the dīkṣa (initiation) name of Śaṅkara Bhagavatpāda where 'Bhagavatpāda' should have been a dīkṣa name or a title given to the saṁnyāsī. The guru then formally started teaching the Vedānta-śāstra to Śaṅkara. A few doubts could arise here. If Śaṅkara was firmly established in the Self, which is the goal of Vedānta, then what was the purpose of learning Vedānta again? Also, wasn't he already well versed in the Vedānta-śāstra during his gurukula days? Yes, he was. However, it must be noted here that varied interpretations of the Upaniṣads and *Brahma-sūtras*, beyond the Advaitic interpretation, existed even before the time of Śaṅkara. Both Śaṅkara and Rāmānuja mention of masters (such as Upavarśa, Ātreya Brahmanandī, Draviḍācārya or Dramiḍācārya, Ācārya Sundarapāṇḍya, Kṛtakoṭi, Bodhāyana, Śrivatsāṅka, Śrivatsāṅka miśra, etc.) in their commentaries. Hence, Śaṅkara wanted a guru who could interpret the Vedānta śāstras in the light of Advaita-vedānta, which is what Govinda Bhagavatpāda, who came in the Advaita-vedānta tradition after Gauḍapāda, imparted to Śaṅkara.

We understand that Śaṅkara remained with the guru for nearly four years. These were the years when Śaṅkara spent all his time in contemplation of the dictums of the Upaniṣads, meditation and absorption in the Self in the caves and on the banks of the river Narmada. It is this intimate relationship of the Ācārya with the river Narmada that is reflected in his *Narmadāṣṭakam*, which, compared to his other stotras on rivers, has more observations on the greatness of the river and the life around it. Also, this intimate relationship, along with the yogic powers he attained, helped him contain the fury of the river when she once flowed furiously, breaking the banks and causing danger to the lives around.

Śaṅkara was now firmly established in the Advaitic truth and exhibited all the qualities of a true Jagadguru! The guru was convinced that Śaṅkara could now propagate the message of the Upaniṣads to the world and re-establish Sanātana-dharma. He, hence, commanded Śaṅkara to embark on writing a commentary on the Upaniṣads and the *Brahma-sūtras* with the Advaitic interpretation, on the lines of what he had taught him. He bade Śaṅkara farewell and asked all his disciples to accompany the young jñānī to Kashi. This was important, as Kashi was one of the foremost seats of learning in Bhārata. Hence, anyone who wished to propagate their ideology, had to present it in Kashi in the assembly of learned men, and win them over. Once accepted in Kashi, the ideology would automatically start spreading far and wide. With his purpose of earthly existence fulfilled, Govinda Bhagavatpāda went to nirvikalpa-samādhi and shed his mortal coils.

A jñāni, though indifferent to all relations in life, cannot get over the mercy shown by the guru in imparting the Ultimate knowledge and helping cross the ocean of saṁsāra. It is this gratitude that we see in many later works of the Ācārya, where he begins by invocation to his guru Govinda.[4] What to say of the guru who imparts all knowledge to the disciple through his immense compassion, and rejoices, without a trace of ego or jealousy, at every accomplishment of the disciple! What to say of the disciple who considers every accomplishment as the grace of the guru and remains ever indebted to him! Such an exemplary guru–śiṣya relationship could be seen between Govinda Bhagavatpāda and Śaṅkara.

ADHYĀYA 5

To the Shining City of Kashi

काश्यां हि काश्यते काशी काशी सर्वप्रकाशिका ।
सा काशी विदिता येन तेन प्राप्ता हि काशिका ॥

Kashi shines in Kashi alone, Kashi spreads light everywhere;
The one who knows that Kashi (i.e., the self) he alone understands the real Kashi.

—*Kāśī-pañcakam* verse 4

It would have indeed been a sight to behold, to see the twelve-year-old jñānī surrounded by many yatis, much older in age, at Kashi. As stated earlier, Govinda Bhagavatpāda's popularity as one of the foremost teachers of Vedānta was already widespread. Moreover, the news of the arrival of his illustrious young disciple would have created waves of excitement and wonder in Kashi. As was the custom, the king of Kashi himself came to receive Śaṅkara and his retinue.

Kashi, being the greatest seat of learning, had scholars from various traditions and schools such as Nyāya, Vaiśeṣika, Sāṅkhya, Yoga, Mīmāṁsā, other schools of Vedānta, Bauddha, Jaina, Kāpālika, Pāśupata, and many more who stayed and taught in Kashi. Thus, this time in Kashi was important for

Śaṅkara to understand the various other schools of thought and traditions and share with them, as well as propagate among the people, the tenets of Advaita-vedānta. People could not hold themselves from being around the young jñānī, drawn by his magnetic personality and divine aura. With many disciples joining the fold, Śaṅkara became Ācārya Śaṅkara! The disciples increased manifold – Citsukha and Sanandana being the chief among them. Citsukha, as stated earlier, was the childhood friend of the Ācārya belonging to the Nambūdiri community, while Sanandana was a Vaiṣṇava who hailed from the Cola-deśa in the South, both of whom joined the Ācārya in Kashi.

While at Kashi, Ācārya was invited to various gurukulas. In one such place, he observed an old man, in the last phase of his life, memorising the grammatical sūtras of Paṇini. Compassion arose in the heart of the Ācārya, and he uttered a set of verses as an upadeśa to destroy one's delusion. These were called *Moha-mudgara* (the pestle for delusion), more popularly known as '*Bhaja Govindam*' because it begins with these words.

One day, after taking a bath in the Ganga, when the Ācārya was walking with his disciples through one of the narrow lanes of Kashi, he saw a Caṇḍāla coming before him with four dogs. One of the disciples asked the Caṇḍāla to move aside and give space for the Ācārya to move forward. The Caṇḍāla however continued to look at the Ācārya and said to him, 'Who do you want to move aside? This body or the soul? The body is inert and hence cannot move anywhere. The soul is present everywhere and hence cannot move anywhere.'

Realising that it was Lord Viśvanātha, the Universal Guru, Himself, who had come as the Caṇḍāla and given this great upadeśa, Ācārya composed five verses (popularly called *Manīṣā-pañcakaṃ*) defining who a real guru is.

Days passed by at Kashi, with Ācārya holding regular lectures expounding the tenets of Advaita-vedānta, which were attended by large crowds of people, laymen and scholars alike. However, the command of his guru to write the commentaries on the Upaniṣads and *Brahma-sūtras* was yet to be completed. Kashi, though a place of high spiritual aura, with all its hustle and bustle, did not seem the right place to accomplish this task. Hence, with a select group of disciples, Ācārya set forth towards Badarikāśrama in the north, where Lord Nārāyaṇa himself is present in the form of a yogī in constant meditation. Vyāsa had composed the *Brahma-sūtras*, the Mahābhārata and the Purāṇas by staying in a cave (called Vyāsa-guhā) in Badarikāśrama, besides the river Sarasvatī. Hence, Śaṅkara felt this place would provide the right inspiration for his commentaries.

ADHYĀYA 6

Towards Deva-bhūmi

अस्त्युत्तरस्यां दिशि देवतात्मा हिमालयो नाम नगाधिराजः ।
पूर्वापरौ तोयनिधी विगाह्य स्थितः पृथिव्या इव मानदण्डः ॥

There, in the northern part (of the country) is the divine lord of mountains called the Himālaya who spanning across the eastern and western oceans appears like the measuring rod of the earth!
—*Kumārasambhavam* 1.1

Ācārya and his disciples travelled along the banks of the Ganga, from Kashi to Haridwar. Haridwar marks the entrance to Deva-bhūmi, the land of the celestials. The disciples were awestruck by the beauty of the snow-clad Himalayas, the unique flora and fauna and the divine Ganga nourishing the entire land. This was indeed a Deva-bhūmi, truly a heaven! From Haridwar, they went to Rishikesh, the sacred land where many sages were performing penance in their subtle bodies. Rishikesh had a temple of Hṛśīkeśa Nārāyaṇa (which is currently called the Bharat mandir) where the vigraha was missing in the sanctum sanctorum and instead a sālagrāma was being worshipped. On enquiry with the local people, it was understood that several years back, during the attack of foreign invaders who were iconoclasts, the vigraha was placed in the riverbed in the fear that the invaders would destroy it! Ācārya was deeply saddened to hear this. Through his yogic powers, he located the vigraha lying inside the Māyā-kuṇḍa and dived in to retrieve it. He consecrated the vigraha in the temple. This indeed brought great joy to the people of Rishikesh. In remembrance of this event, every year a festival is celebrated on the Vasanta (Basant)-pañcamī day, the day when Ācārya is said to have done the consecration by carrying a sālagrāma to the Māyā-kuṇḍa and getting it back to the temple on a palanquin.

Carrying on with their journey, they next travelled to Deva-prayag, where the river Alakanandā coming from Badarinath joins with the river Bhāgīrathī coming from Gaumukh at the foot of the Gangotri glacier, to become Ganga. Further up, they went to Rudra-prayag, where Śiva is said to have sat in penance after the immolation of Satī. Kālidāsa recounts this scene in the *Kumārasambhava*.[1] This is where the river Mandākinī coming from Kedarnath joins with Alakanandā. They then travelled further north to Karna-prayag, where the river Piṇḍārī joins Alakanandā, and Nanda-prayag, where the river Nandākinī joins Alakanandā. They then reached Vishnu-prayag, where the river Dhauli Ganga joins the river Alakanandā. Vishnu-prayag is close to Brahmapura (now called Joshimath), which was the capital of the Katyuri kings who ruled the region. The then Katyuri king, Vāsudev, who had adopted Buddhism, got transformed with the contact of the Ācārya and his upadeśa. He turned into a follower of Sanātana-dharma, and, in later times, he and his descendants were responsible for the construction of many temples in this region. King Vāsudev took care of the Ācārya and the disciples during their entire stay in Badarikāśrama. It was also, probably, the devotion of the king that made Ācārya establish the Uttarāmnāya-maṭha at Joshimath.

Travelling further north, the retinue reached the sacred land of Badarī-Nārāyaṇa. Many consider Lord Badarī-Nārāyaṇa as the kula-devatā (family deity) of the entire Bhārata itself! However, the Ācārya was saddened to see that, like Rishikesh, here again the vigraha of Badarī-Nārāyaṇa was missing, and worship was being done to a sālagrāma. On enquiry with the local elders, a very similar story was heard, of hiding the vigraha inside the Nārada-kuṇḍa in fear of the invaders destroying it. Ācārya once again sat in deep meditation and in a state of trance jumped into the waters of the Nārada-kuṇḍa, much against the advice of the local people warning him against the strong currents of the river. In some time, Ācārya came out with the vigraha of Badarī-Nārāyaṇa. The vigraha was a caturbhuja (four-armed) form seated in a yogic posture. The vigraha was slightly damaged because of remaining in the riverbed for so long. However, Ācārya realised that it was the divine will to have the vigraha as-is and hence consecrated it and codified the pūjā-vidhāna for the same as per Kerala-tantra (See 'A note on Śaṅkara and Tantra'). He also entrusted the worship of Badarī-Nārāyaṇa to a Nambūdiri Brāhmaṇa, who had accompanied the Ācārya in his travel to Badarī, as the chief priest (called Rawal).

The pūjā-vidhāna at Badarinath includes nava-kalaśa-abhiṣeka,[2] nivedya of pāl-pāyasam,[3] Sahasranāma-arcana, etc., which are followed in most Viṣṇu temples of Kerala. Only the Rawalji has the right to touch the vigraha and perform worship to Badarī-Nārāyaṇa. Ācārya is also said to have laid out the selection process of the Nambūdiri for the post of Rawalji, which includes testing the candidate on various śāstras, ability to perform the variousTāntric rituals, lineage of the candidate (e.g., Nambūdiris belonging to the Raghavapuram Sabhayogam), etc. The selection is also to be approved by the kings of Kerala (now the Travancore dynasty) and Badarikāśrama (i.e., the Garhwal dynasty). The procedure, as laid out by the Ācārya, continues to this day uninterrupted! What to say of the devotion of the Nambūdiris and the kings of the Travancore and Garhwal dynasty!

S.S. Saraswati presents few other perspectives on the tradition of chief priests of Badarinath (2015, pp. 552–55).

With the news of the reconsecration of Badarī-Nārāyaṇa spreading, people from different corners of the country began their pilgrimages to behold the sight of their dear Lord! Ācārya then proceeded to the Vyāsa-guhā, where he began work on the commentaries.

ADHYĀYA 7

Establishing the Core of Advaita-vedānta

नत्वा विशुद्धविज्ञानं शङ्करं करुणानिधिम् ।
भाष्यं प्रसन्नगम्भीरं तत्प्रणीतं विभज्यते ॥

Having prostrated to that pure intellect of Śaṅkara, the ocean of mercy, I take my share of (start my work on) his pleasing yet profound commentary!

—*Bhāmati* Introduction

ब्रह्मसत्यं जगन्मिथ्या जीवो ब्रह्मैव नापरः

Brahman is the truth, the world is only a perception, the individual soul is indeed the Brahman itself and not different from it.

—*Bramha-jñānāvalī-mālā* verse 20

As regards the Vedānta-śāstra, the Upaniṣads and *Brahma-sūtras* were already well established as fundamental Vedāntic texts and this is what Govinda Bhagavatpāda had commanded Śaṅkara to write commentaries on. However, the credit goes to Śaṅkara for considering the *Bhagavad*

Gītā also as a text of Vedānta at par with the Upaniṣads and *Brahma-sūtras* and writing an elaborate commentary on the same. While there were many commentaries on the *Gītā* even before Śaṅkara, as is evident from his introduction to the *Gītā-bhāṣya*,[1] there is no evidence of them commenting on *Gītā* as a Vedāntic text. Thenceforth, the Upaniṣads, *Brahma-sūtras* and *Bhagavad Gītā* have together been considered the fundamental texts of Vedānta, popularly referred by the term 'Prasthāna-trayī'.[2] Every later ācārya of Vedānta has felt the need to comment on the Prasthāna-trayī for them to be accepted as an ācārya of Vedānta.

Śāstra is the name given to any science, since it directs, in a systematic and structured way.[3] Every śāstra in our tradition, has a fundamental text which is in the form of 'sūtras' or aphorisms. These sūtras need to adhere to specific rules, which help in keeping the śāstra succinct and yet resourceful.[4] However, with passage of time, the context of the sūtras is lost which makes the śāstra liable for non-interpretation and wrong interpretation. Hence came the need for a detailed commentary (also adhering to specific rules[5]), which is called the 'bhāṣya'. Beyond these, we have other textual forms such as vārtika, karaka, etc. A vārtika, for example, is written to supplement, complement or at times even correct the bhāṣya to strengthen it against the opposing viewpoints. The kārikā, on the other hand, is a short independent work based on the śāstra, written to explain the basics of a doctrine related to the śāstra. For most śāstras, we would see a sūtra text followed by its bhāṣya and supplemented by the vārtika. The composers of these are referred to as the sūtrakāra, bhāṣyakāra and vārtikakāra for that śāstra. For example, in case of vyākaraṇa- śāstra or grammar, we have Pāṇini as the sūtrakāra, Patañjali as the bhāṣyakāra and Kātyāyana as the vārtikakāra. In the case of Vedānta-śāstra, we have Vyāsa, the composer of the *Brahmā-sūtras* as the sūtrakāra and Śaṅkara (followed by later ācāryas) as bhāṣyakāra. For Advaita-vedānta, Sureśvara, the disciple of Śaṅkara, is considered the vārtikakāra as he composed the vārtika for the *Taittirīya-upaniṣad* and *Bṛhadāraṇyaka-upaniṣad-bhāṣyas* of Śaṅkara.

It is also interesting to see that though there have been commentaries on the Upaniṣads, *Brahma-sūtras* and Bhagavad Gītā before Śaṅkara, as revealed in the works of Śaṅkara and Vyāsa, none of those works are extant today. The commentaries of Śaṅkara are the oldest surviving works we have on the Prasthāna-trayī. It is possible that the work of Śaṅkara became so popular even then that it overshadowed the extant work in his times, which then slowly moved into oblivion.

As regards the Upaniṣads, Śaṅkara chose to comment on eleven of the Upaniṣads – *Īśa, Kena, Kaṭha, Praśna, Muṇḍaka, Māṇḍukya, Taittirīya, Aitareya, Chāndogya, Bṛhadāraṇyaka,* and *Nṛsiṁha* (Pūrva and Uttara) *Tāpani*. The first ten of these are commonly referred to as 'daśopaniṣad', and this seems to have been a selection of the Ācārya itself (from the large corpus of Upaniṣadic literature that existed) based on the criteria that the Upaniṣad did not have any theistic tradition associated with them. The *Nṛsiṁha-tāpani-upaniṣad* is the only exception to this. The commentary on this Upaniṣad seems to have happened later, which we shall deal with in the next chapters.

As stated earlier (see Adhyāya #2: The Divine Descent), Ācārya must have begun his work on the daśopaniṣads with the *Taittirīya-upaniṣad* of the *Taittirīya-yajurveda* branch to which he belonged. He then must have proceeded with the other two Upaniṣads belonging to *Yajurveda*, i.e., *Kaṭha* and *Bṛhadāraṇyaka*, because, in the commentaries on these three Upaniṣads alone, Ācārya has begun with an introduction explaining the meaning of the term Upaniṣad and its purpose. In the commentaries on the daśopaniṣad, Ācārya also give references from three other Upaniṣads outside the daśopaniṣad group, viz., *Śvetāśvatara*, *Kauṣītakī-brāhmaṇa* and *Jābāla*.

The unique aspect of the commentaries of Ācārya, amongst many others, is his conviction of the absolute authority of the Vedas. While later ācāryas have had to take references from outside the Prasthāna-trayī such as the Purāṇas, Śaṅkara, when commenting on the Prasthāna-trayī, primarily gives references from within the Prasthāna-trayī itself and seldom outside.

Beyond these, Ācārya also wrote commentaries on the *Viṣṇu-sahasranāma* and *Sanat-sujātīyam* from the Mahābhārata, which brought forth his profound study and understanding of the Itihāsas and Purāṇas as well. Ācārya had fulfilled the wishes of his guru and established the Advaita-siddhānta through his commentaries, which could now provide the much-needed light and direction to the seekers of truth. All this was accomplished in a period of three–four years! Ācārya was all of sixteen years then!

All this while, Sanandana was devotedly serving the Ācārya and the entire group of disciples. However, some felt that Ācārya had a soft corner for Sanandana. To clear the misconception, one day when Sanandana was washing clothes on the other bank of the Ganga, Ācārya called out loud to him. As soon as he heard the voice of the guru, without wasting a second and without being mindful of where he was, Sanandana started walking towards the Ācārya across the river Ganga! People on either side were shouting aloud trying to stop Sanandana. But Sanandana seemed to hear nothing. He just knew that he had to be beside his guru at the earliest to listen to his command. When the grace of the guru can save a person from drowning in the ocean of saṁsāra, can he drown in a mere physical body of water? At every step that Sanandana placed, there blossomed a lotus helping him cross the river safely! Such was his guru-bhakti. This put an end to the misunderstandings of the other disciples, and they recognised the greatness of Sanandana. Seeing this, Ācārya's joy knew no bounds and he lovingly called Sanandana as 'Padmapāda', the lotus footed!

Occasionally, King Vāsudev also made a visit to the Ācārya, listened to his lectures on Advaita and sought his blessings. In a few days, bidding farewell to the land of Badari, Ācārya and the disciples visited Kedarnath, had the darśan of Kedāreśvara, visited Gangotri and Yamunotri and then moved to Uttara-Kashi. Uttara-Kashi has been considered, even in the Purāṇas, as a land of penance, and Ācārya wished to spend some time in this place on the banks of the river Ganga, contemplating on the truths of the Upaniṣads.

A Note on the Advaita-vedānta of Śaṅkara

Advaita-vedānta of Śaṅkara is but the Advaita-vedānta of the Upaniṣads, the *Brahma-sūtras*, Bhagavad Gītā and that of all the ācāryas of the Advaita paramparā starting from Nārāyaṇa until Gauḍapāda and Govinda Bhagavatpāda. This section aims to present this siddhānta in a nutshell as seen from the works of the Ācārya.

- Everyone wishes to be happy and ward off sorrow, isn't it?
- What causes sorrow? Vedānta says that the true cause of sorrow is misplaced identity - the fact that we consider ourselves as different things (i.e., the body, mind, intellect, caste, religion, gender, social position, etc.) - everything except our true nature.
- What is our true nature? This is the journey that Vedānta takes us through. It finally reaches the conclusion that our true nature is the very life principle that is pulsating within us. That very life principle which is the source of all creation and has filled the entire universe. It is of the nature of Existence, Consciousness, Bliss (Sat-Cit-Ānanda). The Upaniṣads refer to it as Brahman!
- How do we know this is our true nature? We experience it everyday when we go into deep sleep (dreamless sleep). However, we are not able to recollect it later because of the lack of any sensory experience there. The Upaniṣads bring this to our notice and that is how we come to know of it.
- Why do we not know it this very moment? Because we are habituated to understanding ourselves as different

things, with varied indentities. How can we see the bottom of the lake if the water is muddy and with lot of ripples? The false identities are caused because of a primeval ignorance in us, which is called variedly as ajñāna, avidyā or māyā.

- What is the nature of this avidyā or māyā? It is indescribable because none can really comprehend it. It is indeed the power of Brahman itself that veils our true nature and projects wrong identities on the same.[6]

Many accuse Gauḍapāda and Śaṅkara of being Māyāvādīs, i.e., introducing the 'so-called' confusing concept of Māyā, propagating it and in essence, escaping the queries of the opponent philosophies by stating that this Māyā is inexplicable. This misunderstanding ought to be cleared. The term Māyā appears at least thirty times in the *Ṛgveda* in various contexts. In some cases, it is used to refer to the power of the Asuras[7] while in some, it is simply used to indicate the power of the deity[8] and so on. *Bṛhadāraṇyaka-upaniṣad* speaks of Indra creating the world using his power of Māyā.[9] *Śvetāśvatara-upaniṣad*[10] explains Māyā as prakṛti and Lord as the Māyin, i.e., the one who possesses the power of Māyā. Kṛṣṇa Himself speaks of his power as Māyā which keeps the people stuck in the world of birth and death, which can be crossed only through His grace.[11] Thus, we see that the concept of Māyā has been existing right from Vedic times and is not a figment of imagination by Gauḍapāda or Śaṅkara.

- How will this avidyā or māyā end? When we know our true nature as Brahman. Just like when light comes, darkness automatically goes away.
- How can we know our true nature? There are various methods and approaches that Vedānta takes us through. However, we first need to cultivate the necessary qualifications to be eligible for this. These are (1) discrimation between temporary and permanent (2) renunciation, i.e., giving up on the fruits of all actions (3) developing the six qualities of sensory control, mental control, self-withdrawal, forbearance, faith (in śāstras and guru), and self-settledness (4) intense desire to be liberated from this mundane world and know our true nature.
- What is the benefit of doing all this and knowing our true nature as Brahman? Knowing that our true nature is happiness, we will not be affected by the vagaries of the external world, even as we continue to function in the world. That would be the most beautiful way to live! Such as person is called 'jīvan-mukta'.

ADHYĀYA 8

The Approval of Vyāsa

शङ्करं शङ्कराचार्यं केशवं बादरायणं सूत्रभाष्यकृतौ वन्दे भगवन्तौ पुनः पुनः ।

Śaṅkarācārya is Śaṅkara (Śiva) himself and Bādarāyaṇa is Keśava (Viṣṇu) himself, I prostrate again and again to both – the composer of the sūtra and bhāṣya (on Vedānta) respectively.

—Traditional verse

One day, during the Ācārya's stay at Uttara-kashi, an old Brāhmaṇa came to meet him. He had heard of the popularity of the Ācārya's commentary on the *Brahma-sūtras* and wanted to meet him to both congratulate on this great work and clarify some of his doubts. The clarification sought was on the sutra 3.1.1,[1] which speaks of the transmigration of the soul from one body to another. The conversation between the Ācārya and the Brāhmaṇa continued for a very long time. The depth of questions and standard of arguments raised by the Brāhmaṇa convinced the Ācārya that this was no ordinary Brāhmaṇa. Satisfied with the explanations of the Ācārya on the questions raised, the Brāhmaṇa revealed his true form as Vyāsa, the author of the *Brahma-sūtras* Himself!

This was indeed the greatest validation to the commentary of the Ācārya!

It is said that the Ācārya was initially destined only for a life of sixteen years, which was coming to an end. Hence, Vyāsa blessed Ācārya with another sixteen years of life so that he could spread the message of Advaita-vedānta that he had so profoundly established through his bhāṣyas. Vyāsa also mentioned to Śaṅkara that to spread the message of Advaita-vedānta, he needs to counter the arguments raised by the mīmāṁsakas (ritualists) who, by then, had effectively countered the spread of Buddhism and Jainism and quite firmly established the 'karma-kāṇḍa' (ritualistic section) of the Vedas. Having thus blessed Śaṅkara, Vyāsa returned leaving him with a sense of blessedness, gratitude and fulfilment.

Kumārila Bhaṭṭa (reverently called Bhaṭṭapāda), who lived in Prayag, was the chief proponent of mīmāṁsā in Bhārata.[2] Hence, it was now important for Śaṅkara to convince Bhaṭṭapāda of the superiority of the Advaita-vedānta over mīmāṁsā, which would then pave the way for wider propagation of the Vedānta.

Bhaṭṭapāda had rendered a yeomen service in preventing the decline of Vedic dharma by stopping the spread of Buddhism.

As far as the mīmāṁsā-śāstra is concerned, the fundamental texts are the *Mīmāṁsā-sūtras* of Jaimini, *Sūtra-bhāṣya* by Śabara-svāmī and *Vṛtti* by Upavarṣa. On these, Bhaṭṭapāda had composed several works such as *vivaraṇa, śloka-vārtika, Tantra-vārtika*, and *ṭup-ṭīkā*, which are considered reference texts for study of mīmāṁsā even till today.

To be able to better counter the Buddhist masters, Bhaṭṭapāda disguised himself as a Buddhist, enrolled as a student with them and understood the tenets of Buddhism thoroughly. During one of the lectures where the Buddhist masters were heavily criticising the Vedas, Bhaṭṭapāda could not hold back his tears. Noticing this, the masters understood that he was a Vaidika under the guise of a Buddhist. They immediately ordered for him to be pushed from atop a mountain cliff! The religion of the Buddha, who was a paragon of love, compassion and non-violence, had degenerated to this level of hatred and violence! Owing to his unshakeable faith in the Vedas, Bhaṭṭapāda escaped the tragedy with minimal injuries. He then summoned the Buddhist masters for open debates and countered them ferociously till they accepted defeat. Thus, in a way, he, his peers and his disciples had created the right fertile ground for the tree of Vedānta to grow.

ADHYĀYA 9

The Debate with Maṇḍana

वदन्तु शास्त्राणि यजन्तु देवान् कुर्वन्तु कर्माणि भजन्तु देवताः।
आत्मैक्यबोधेन विनापि मुक्तिर्न सिध्यति ब्रह्मशतान्तरेऽपि ॥

Let scriptures be quoted, yajñas and karmas be performed, deities be worshipped, without the realisation of one's identity with the Ātman, there is no liberation even in the lifetime of a hundred Brahmas put together.

—*Viveka-cūḍāmaṇi* verse 6

The Ācārya began his journey towards Prayag along with his disciples to meet Bhaṭṭapāda. They travelled along the banks of the Yamuna visiting Kurukshetra, Mathura and Vrindavan. The Ācārya prostrated at each of these places that had witnessed the childhood pranks of Kṛṣṇa. The dark waters of Yamuna made him think if the waters had become dark by Kṛṣṇa constantly bathing in them?[1]

As they travelled towards Prayag, they saw many people returning from there. On enquiry, they understood that Bhaṭṭapāda was self-immolating on a pyre of husk. Betraying one's teacher was considered a sin and Bhaṭṭapāda had betrayed the Buddhist masters by hiding his identity and learning the Buddhist tenets from them. Knowing that Bhaṭṭapāda's mortal coil would fall off soon, Ācārya rushed to take the darśan of the great Vaidika. On reaching, he paid his respects and announced the intent of his arrival. Bhaṭṭapāda had already heard a lot about the greatness of Śaṅkara. As he was in his last moments, Bhaṭṭapāda was in no mind for a debate. He instead requested the Ācārya to meet his disciple Maṇḍana Miśra, who lived in Māhiśmatī, and have the debate with him. This would fulfil Ācārya's purpose.

Bhaṭṭapāda had two prominent disciples, Maṇḍana and Prabhākara. While Maṇḍana followed the same ideology as Bhaṭṭapāda, Prabhākara differed in a few respects. In addition, *Vidhi-viveka*, the work of Maṇḍana on mīmāṁsā, is considered a great reference for study of mīmāṁsā. It was, probably for this reason, that Bhaṭṭapāda suggested Maṇḍana for the debate with Śaṅkara.

Finally, like the Ṛṣis of yore,[2] Bhaṭṭapāda requested the Ācārya to enlighten him in the last moments of his life, so that he may realise his true nature and attain liberation. Being a true Vaidika all his life, Bhaṭṭapāda had attained the necessary purity of mind and was in such a mature state that, as the Ācārya enunciated the supreme truths of the Upaniṣads, Bhaṭṭapāda immediately turned inwards, got established in the Self and went into nirvikalpa-samādhi. He then became oblivious to his physical existence and the pain it was going through, even as the fire kept consuming the body away! Having witnessed the liberation of Bhaṭṭapāda, as suggested by him, the Ācārya and his disciples started walking towards Māhiśmatī on the banks of the river Narmada. He was now returning to the land of Narmada after nearly four years, when he bade farewell to his guru!

Maṇḍana Miśra, also known as Viśvarūpa, was a Gauḍa-Brāhmaṇa born as the son of Hima-mitra, who served as the royal preceptor to the King of Kashmir. Viśvarūpa had his upbringing in Kashmir, which was well known as the intellectual centre of Bhārata. He was given in marriage to Sarasvatī (or Sarasavāṇī), who was the daughter of Viṣṇu Mitra from the land of the river Son (probably in modern-day Madhya Pradesh). After marriage, the couple stayed in Kashmir for some time before shifting to Māhiśmatī. Sarasvatī was also called Ubhaya-Bhāratī as she was well versed in both pūrva-mīmāṁsā and uttara-mīmāṁsā.

On reaching Māhiśmatī, Śaṅkara enquires about the house of Maṇḍana. He is informed that where even the parrots discuss the mīmāṁsā-sūtras is the house of Maṇḍana! The retinue reached their destination and, incidentally that day, Maṇḍana was observing certain śrāddha (related to the manes) ceremonies at his house. Maṇḍana was not too happy seeing a person in ochre robes at his doorstep since that reminded him of the Buddhist bhikkus who were responsible for the decline of the Vedic dharma. Nevertheless, the guest was welcomed with respect by both Maṇḍana and Sarasvatī and offered food (anna-bhikśa). However, Śaṅkara made it clear to Maṇḍana that he had come not for anna-bhikṣā but vāda-bhikṣā (i.e., alms in the form of debate). Maṇḍana agreed and the very next day, a debate was arranged between Śaṅkara and Maṇḍana in the presence of great scholars of the times. The condition of the debate was that the one losing it would need to adopt the āśrama (lifestyle) of the other, i.e., Maṇḍana would adopt saṁnyāsa and Śaṅkara would adopt the life of a householder, respectively. The debate needed a judge who could decide victory and defeat. Interestingly, Śaṅkara requested Sarasvatī, the wife of Maṇḍana, to be the judge of the debate. He knew that she was well versed in both pūrva-mīmāṁsā and uttara-mīmāṁsā and believed that she would do justice to the position of a judge without any bias. Though we have instances of women scholars debating and discussing in the Upaniṣads, such as Gārgī and Maitreyī, this was probably the first known instance of a woman occupying the position of a judge!

The debate began and continued for days. Maṇḍana argued that mīmāṁsā was the true purport of the Vedas as they spoke of actions/karma and that the Upaniṣads were just flowery literature speaking of some esoteric philosophy without any action and substance.[3] Śaṅkara on the other hand argued that the Upaniṣads alone were the goal of the Vedas and that mīmāṁsā was only a step in the direction towards creating a pure mind that can progress to the bigger goal. It was not an end in itself.[4] Very soon, Maṇḍana found himself cornered with no definitive arguments to counter the views of Śaṅkara. He was also taken in by the brilliance and personality of the Ācārya. Even before the result, Maṇḍana had mentally accepted the Ācārya as his guru. Sarasvatī, being the fair judge, realised the supremacy of Śaṅkara's views and declared him the winner of the debate. Both Maṇḍana and Sarasvatī prostrated in front of the Ācārya, who graciously accepted Maṇḍana as his disciple, initiated him into saṁnyāsa and gave him the name 'Sureśvara', the lord of the celestials! This created huge ripples in the mīmāṁsā circles as they had lost two of their major proponents – Bhaṭṭapāda had ended his life and now Maṇḍana accepted saṁnyāsa!

ADHYĀYA 10

To the Sacred Mount of Śiva

सेवे श्रीगिरि मल्लिकार्जुनं महालिङ्गं शिवालिङ्गितम्

Worship lord Mallikārjuna at Śrī Parvata, that huge liṅga eternally embraced by Umā.

—*Śivānandalaharī* verse 50

Śaṅkara accompanied by Sureśvara, Sarasvatī, Padmapāda, Citsukha, and other disciples, started his journey from Māhiśmatī towards Cālukya-deśa (modern-day Maharashtra). This region had a predominance of Śaiva bhakti with prevalent traditions of Khāṇḍoba, Mhālsā, Nāth tradition, etc. There was also a dominant Śākta tradition centred around temples, such as Mahālakṣmī of Kolhapur, Bhavānī of Tulajapur, Renukā of Mahur, Saptaśṛṅgī of Vani, Ekavīrā of Karla, Ambajogai and many more Śaktī shrines. The Vaiṣṇava tradition was primarily around Viṭṭhala of Pandharpur. Śaṅkara visited many of these places including Panchavati on the banks of the river Godavari near Nasik, which was the land sanctified by the penance of many sages and the stay of Lord Rāma, Sītā and Lakṣmaṇa. He also visited Pandharpur where he composed the famous *Pāṇḍuraṅgāṣṭakam* on Lord Viṭṭhala. Herein, he describes the unique form of Viṭṭhala standing on a brick with arms akimbo.[1] He then visited the five Jyotirliṅga kṣetras of Tryambakeshwar,[2] Bhimashankar,[3] Ghrishneshwar,[4] Naganath[5] and Vaidyanath.[6] Then, having crossed the rivers Tapti and Godavari, he headed towards that sacred mount of Śiva, Srisailam, on the banks of the river Krishna in modern-day Andhra Pradesh.

Srisailam has been a significant place in the life of the Ācārya and is closely connected with some of his most important works and events.

Srisailam, from time immemorial, has been a great Śaiva and Śākta centre where different forms of Śaiva tradition including Kāpālika, Pāśupata, etc., have thrived. We can still see many caves in and around Srisailam, such as Bhairava Sela, where people worship Bhairava, the deity of the Kāpālikas. There are also many sculptures found near Srisailam of Lakulīśa who is considered the proponent of the Pāśupata cult. Srisailam was the place where Arjuna sat in meditation towards Śiva to obtain the Pāśupata-astra. Śiva came in the guise of a kirāta (hunter), had a duel with Arjuna and finally blessed him with the Pāśupata-astra. Arjuna is said to have worshipped Śiva here with jasmine flowers (mallikā) and hence the Lord is called Mallikārjuna. The son born to Śiva and Pārvatī, while they were in the form of kirātas, is called variedly as kirāta-sūnu or Veṭṭaikku-oru-makan and is a popular diety worshipped especially in Kerala. Interestingly, Veṭṭaikku-oru-makan is also the family deity of Āryāmbā and his temple still exists in the premises of the Melpāzhūr mana! Srisailam is also one of the 51 Śaktī pīṭhas where the Goddess is worshipped as Bhramarāmbikā on whom Ācārya composed the *Bhramarāmbā-aṣṭakam*.

Ācārya stayed at Srisailam for a long time as he was drawn in by the spiritually vibrant atmosphere of the place. It is here that he composed three of his popular works – *Śivānandalaharī*, *Saundaryalaharī* and *Yoga-tārāvalī*. Very rarely do we see a mention of places in the devotional works of the Ācārya unless they are composed on the deities of that place. In *Yoga-tārāvalī*,[7] he yearns for going into samādhi in one of the caves in Srisailam. In *Śivānandalaharī*,[8] he mentions the place and the deities and calls the liṅga here as Mahāliṅga, which is tightly embraced by Pārvatī.[9]

Ācārya regularly gave discourses and people were drawn in huge numbers to attend these. Attracted by both the personality of the Ācārya and the simplicity of the Upaniṣadic truths, many, even from other theistic faiths, adopted the path of Vedānta. This irked some of the theistic groups, such as the kāpālikas who were aggressive worshippers of Śiva and practised various non-Vedic approaches like worshipping with meat, wine, etc. One such kāpālika, named Ugra-bhairava, came to the Ācārya in the guise of a believer and when no one was around, told the Ācārya that worship to his deity Bhairava would only be complete if he offered the head of a great jñānī like the Ācārya. He hence requested Ācārya if he could take him to his cave where they could behead the Ācārya and offer that to Bhairava! What a weird request this was! However, a krānta-darśī (perceiver beyond time) that the Ācārya was, he smilingly accepted the request, but suggested that the kāpālika should come in the middle of the night when all the disciples would have gone to sleep. The kāpālika came as suggested and took the Ācārya to a distant cave. As the kāpālika was preparing for the sacrifice, Ācārya withdrew his senses, established them in his mind, merged his mind into his self and remained firmly established as the self-absorbed in nirvikalpa-samādhi. At the same time, Padmapāda suddenly woke up from sleep feeling some concern for the Ācārya. His fear was proved right when he did not find the Ācārya around. He began his search and soon landed up at the cave.

Just as the kāpālika was about to behead the Ācārya, a strange roar of a lion was heard in the cave. Before the kāpālika and his members could understand what happened, they saw a lion roaring, jumping upon them and tearing them apart. In some time, as Ācārya opened his eyes, he saw a lot of bloodshed around him. He saw Ugra-bhairava and many other kāpālikas lying dead on the ground and being torn to pieces. He also saw Padmapāda there who was standing there in a possessed state. Ācārya understood what had transpired. Lord Nṛsiṁha, who was Padmapāda's iṣṭa-devatā, had manifested in him, put an end to the kāpālikas and saved Ācārya's life.

Padmapāda, before accepting saṁnyāsa, was a Vaiṣṇava and great devotee of Lord Nṛsiṁha. Once, with a definite resolve to have the vision of Nṛsiṁha, he retired to the forest and started intensely meditating using the Nṛsiṁha mantra. Several days passed and he could not get the vision. Seeing him dejected, a hunter came by and asked him the reason.

He asked Padmapāda to describe the appearance of Nṛsiṁha. When Padmapāda told him that it was half man and half lion, the hunter told him, 'I have been born and brought up in this forest but have never seen such an animal here before. You are a guest in my forest, and I cannot see you dejected. I promise to find the animal you are looking for and bring it by end of the day today else I will put an end to myself!' The hunter started his search intently but of no avail. Finally, when the end of day reached and he was about to end his life, Lord Nṛsiṁha appeared. The hunter rejoiced at this and chaining Nṛsiṁha took him to Padmapāda. While the hunter could very well see and feel Nṛsiṁha, Padmapāda couldn't. He however could hear him and Lord Nṛsiṁha told him that his devotion lacked the intensity of the hunter and hence he couldn't have the vision. However, Nṛsiṁha promised Padmapāda that he would always be with him and manifest at the appropriate moment.

To pacify this Nṛsiṁha-āveśa (possession) in Padmapāda, Ācārya composed the *Lakṣmī-nṛsiṁha-karāvalamba-stotram*. Ācārya is also said to have written the commentary on the *Nṛsiṁha-pūrva* and *uttara-tāpani-upaniṣad* during this time.

ADHYĀYA 11

Arrival of the 'Realised Śiṣya'

प्रकाशयन्ते परमात्मतत्त्वं करस्थधात्रीफलवद्यदेकं श्लोकास्तु हस्तामलकाः
प्रसिद्धास्तत्कर्तुराख्यापि तथैव वृत्ता

As the knowledge of the Self was natural to him like an Āmalaka (gooseberry) fruit in one's hand, he became famous under the name of Hastāmalaka.

— *Madhavīya-śaṅkara-vijaya* 12.57

After staying for some time in Srisailam, Ācārya proceeded to the holy land of Gokarna on the west coast where the Lord is called Mahābaleśvara.

Rāvaṇa once received the ātma-liṅga from Śiva when he visited Kailāsa. While taking it back to Lanka, to perform his daily ablutions, he placed the liṅga on the ground. After his ablutions, as he tried to pick up the liṅga, he couldn't do so as it had got deeply rooted at this place and wouldn't come out even with the best of efforts. All the efforts made by Rāvaṇa to uproot the liṅga deformed it into the shape of the cow's ear and hence the name Gokarna. This is also why the Lord here is called Mahābaleśvara – the strongest one. This place also marks the beginning of Paraśurāma kṣetra, the land that

Paraśurāma reclaimed from the sea by throwing his axe into it. Ācārya is also said to have established a maṭha at a place called Aśoke near Gokarna about which we shall see later (see Adhyāya #17: Tradition of Śaṅkara).

After staying in meditation for a few days in Gokarna, he travelled to Harihar where the deity is present as Śaṅkara-Nārāyaṇa. Here, he gave the message to the people on the oneness of Śiva and Viṣṇu. He mentioned that any debates or arguments on the superiority of Śiva or Viṣṇu, and the subsequent hatred amongst the followers, is completely futile. He then proceeded to the beautiful Kuṭakācala or Kutajādri hills that was sanctified by the penance of several sages such as Kola (hence the name Kolāpuri or Kollur). Ācārya came here specifically to worship the rare mithuna-liṅga, called so because it represented both Śiva and Śaktī. The liṅga also had a golden line dividing it into two unequal sections – the left bigger section representing the three Śaktīs, Durgā, Lakṣmī and Sarasvatī, and right smaller section representing the trinity, Brahmā, Viṣṇu and Śiva.[1] Having taken a bath at the sacred and therapeutic Sauparṇikā river and worshiped the mithuna-liṅga, he meditated here for many days atop the peaks of the Kutajādri hills. In his meditation, he had a vision of the Supreme in the form of the Divine Mother with four hands holding the śaṅkha, cakra, displaying the abhaya-mudra and varada-mudra, and seated in padmāsana. In line with his vision, he got a vigraha made and consecrated the same on top of a Śrī-cakra. This is the vigraha of Goddess Mūkāmbikā that we see today. He then codified the pūjā-vidhāna in line with the āgamas and Kerala-tantra.

During his stay at Mookambika, one day the Ācārya was physically not feeling well. It is said that the Goddess came in the form of a young girl and offered him a kaṣāya (āyurvedic concoction) that cured the Ācārya. In remembrance of this, Ācārya instructed for the kaṣāya to be prepared daily as nivedya for the last pūjā (called attāzha pūjā) and offered to all devotees to relieve them of their sufferings. The place where the Ācārya meditated is called Śaṅkara-pīṭham and is situated in the southwest corner of the sanctum sanctorum. During his stay here, it was customary for the Ācārya to be invited by the nearby Brāhmaṇa villages (also called agrahāra because there were temples of Hari or Hara or both at the end of each village) for bhikṣā, during which people had a darśan of the Ācārya and listened to his upadeśa. During a visit to one such village nearby, called Śrī-Bali, a Brāhmaṇa named Prabhākara approached the Ācārya with his son who seemed to neither speak nor hear nor understand anything from childhood.

Scholars opine that the child would have been yoga-braṣṭa (a yogī who didn't attain realisation in that birth) in its previous birth, as Kṛṣṇa says in the Gītā, and hence born as a jñāni in this birth.[2] This also reminds us of the story of jaḍa-bharata from the *Bhāgavata Purāṇa* who attained realisation after multiple births.

The moment Ācārya saw the child, he experienced an unknown happiness. Looking into his eyes, the Ācārya asked, 'Who are you child? Who are your parents? Where are you coming from? What's your name? You bring so much happiness to me. Speak O child!'[3] The incident reminds us of similar questions asked by Govinda Bhagavatpāda to the young Śaṅkara! Though these seem like mundane questions, when coming from mahātmas, it has a very different purpose. These questions were a trigger for that great soul to express itself. For the first time since birth, the child spoke, and uttered a set of twelve verses (popularly known as *Hastāmalaka Stotra* or *Hastāmalakīyam*), the essence of which was that it's true nature was the ātman that is eternally present.[4] Ācārya told the Brāhmaṇa, 'This child is a jñānī. While he has uttered these beautiful verses here, the moment you take him home and try to engage him in worldly activities, he will again go back to his dumb and deaf state. He would be of no use to you. Hence it would be better if you hand him over to me.' Prabhākara was experiencing mixed emotions – he was excited that his child spoke and that too a set of poetic verses, but he was shocked to hear Ācārya's request and finally in a state of acceptance and sadness, he handed over the child to the Ācārya and left the place. Ācārya accepted the child as his disciple and named him Hastāmalaka because he knew the truth as clear as a gooseberry (āmalaka) on one's palm (hasta). While the other disciples wrote commentaries and explanations on Ācārya's work, Hastāmalaka had the unique distinction of the Ācārya writing a commentary (*Hastāmalakīya-bhāṣya*) on Hastāmalaka's work! The guru writing a commentary on the work of his śiṣya! What to say of the humility of that great guru Śaṅkara who is rightfully called Jagadguru, not only because he is a universal guru but also because he considers the entire universe as his guru!

After staying at Mookambikafor a few days, the Ācārya travelled to the temple of Subrahmaṇya (in Kukke) on the banks of the river Kumāradhāra, where Lord Subrahmaṇya is present in the form of a snake. Ācārya spent a few days in meditation there and proceeded to Sringeri.

ADHYĀYA 12

In the land of Ṛṣyaśṛṅga

यत्राधुनाऽप्युत्तममृष्यशृङ्गस्तपश्चरत्यात्मभृदन्तरङ्गः
संस्पर्शमात्रेण वितीर्णभद्रा विद्योतते यत्र च तुङ्गभद्रा

Where, even today, the great seer Ṛṣyaśṛṅga is practicing penance dissolved in the Supreme Self, where shines the river Tungabhadrā which brings auspiciousness to one who merely touches it (such is the holy land of Sringeri).

— *Madhavīya-śaṅkara-vijaya* 12.64

Sringeri had a special place in the heart of the Ācārya right from the time he experienced the sanctity of the place, as an eight-year-old boy, during his onward journey to Omkareshwar. Ācārya was thrilled to come back to this sacred land of Ṛṣyaśṛṅga after nearly fifteen–sixteen years. It is probably here that, foreseeing the future perils that could once again threaten the sustenance and survival of Sanātana-dharma, Ācārya had the saṅkalpa of establishing monastic institutions (called Āmnāya-maṭhas) at the four corners of Bhārata for the propagation and sustenance of Sanātana-dharma. He began with establishing Sringeri as the southern (dakṣiṇa) Āmnāya-maṭha on the banks of the river Tunga. It must be noted that, except for the Malahānikareśvara temple (which was the Śiva-liṅga worshipped by sage Vibhāṇḍaka), there were no temples in Sringeri then. Ācārya decided to have Goddess Śāradā, the bestower of Supreme knowledge, as the deity in the Sringeri-maṭha.

At that time, the only known temple of Śāradā was in Kashmir,[1] where she was worshipped by the sages, seers and the common people as the form of the Supreme knowledge (Brahma-vidyā-svarūpiṇī). Hence, Ācārya felt it apt to have Śāradā as the deity, since the ultimate objective of the Āmnāya-maṭha was to guide the earnest seekers towards the ultimate knowledge. Now, how was the form of Śāradā in Kashmir? The only one who would know this in detail would be Sureśvara who hailed from Kashmir. Hence, it is very much possible that Sureśvara was instrumental in deciding the form of Śāradā to be consecrated at Sringeri.

The form of the Goddess consecrated was with four hands holding sudhā-kumbha (pot of immortality), akṣamālā (rosary), pustaka (book), and cin-mudrā and seated in padmāsanā. Ācārya also established four protector deities in the four corners of Sringeri – Kālikāmbā to the north, Bhairava to the east, Durgāmbā to the south, and Māruti to the west. These were consecrated to protect the maṭha and the people of Sringeri from all perils – natural and man-made. He then placed Sureśvara as the first Ācārya of this maṭha.

There is also a view that the original Dakṣiṇāmnāya-maṭha established by the Ācārya was in Kudali (near Sringeri) at the confluence of rivers Tunga and Bhadra. The form of Śāradā here, is in a standing posture holding the akṣamālā, a white lotus, Abhaya mudrā and pustaka in her four hands. (See section on 'Kūḍali Sringeri Mahāsaṁsthāna').

While at Sringeri, a young boy named Giri, greatly attracted and devoted to the Ācārya, joined the retinue. He was not as intellectually capable as the other disciples but his devotion to the Ācārya was supreme. He served not just the Ācārya, but the whole retinue of disciples and took care of all their needs. Ācārya would conduct Vedānta sessions every day for the disciples and Giri would devotedly listen to the same, though he understood less of it. One day, Ācārya did not begin the session even past the stipulated time, as Giri had not yet arrived. This irked some of the disciples who casually remarked that Giri's presence added little value to the session anyway. This deeply saddened the Ācārya who immediately went into a trance and, as if in a jiffy, transferred the entire knowledge of Vedānta to Giri who was washing clothes a few miles away. Giri felt a strange power in him. Soon, the disciples were astonished to see an exuberant Giri coming at a distance. He was dancing and singing a beautiful set of verses in praise of his guru who had shown so much compassion to him.[2] These were the eight verses set in Toṭaka metre, and hence popularly called *Toṭakāṣṭaka*. Ācārya embraced Giri and named him 'Toṭaka' after the verses he composed in that metre.

While the Ācārya had a uniform approach towards all his disciples, he knew the strengths of each one of them. One day, the Ācārya called on Sureśvara to write a commentary on his *Brahma-sūtra-bḥāṣya*. While Sureśvara initially hesitated to accept this, unsure of his capability and qualification to do so, he accepted it as he had complete faith in the Ācārya and his decision. However, this created some discontent among the other disciples, especially Padmapāda. Padmapāda was of the view that Sureśvara, having been a strong proponent of rituals in his previous life, would not interpret Vedānta and the commentaries of the Ācārya correctly. This would blemish the credibility of the Ācārya. Coming to know of this, Ācārya called on Sureśvara and asked him to first compose an independent work explaining the tenets of Advaita-vedānta.[3] This resulted in the composing of Sureśvara's monumental work *Naiṣkarmya-siddhi*, wherein he explained the tenets of Advaita as clear as a crystal. Padmapāda himself was amazed to see the clarity of thought and the conviction Sureśvara had in Advaita-vedānta. This also put to rest the concerns of Padmapāda. In parallel, Padmapāda, having obtained the consent of the Ācārya, wrote his commentary on the Śaṅkara-bhāṣya for the first four *Brahma-sūtra*s (including the *adhyāsa-bhāṣya*). He showed them to the Ācārya, who was very much pleased and commended Padmapāda for the work.

However, Padmapāda felt extremely bad that he had doubted the credibility of Sureśvara. This troubled him so much that he even felt embarrassed to face Sureśvara. He finally decided to go on a pilgrimage for a few months, as he believed that would heal his guilt and bring him more peace. Ācārya was not in favour of this as he saw some imminent danger to the life of Padmapāda in this journey. However, Padmapāda was insistent and hence the Ācārya conceded with his request. Ācārya sent along another disciple to be an aid to Padmapāda in this journey.

Padmapāda travelled to many temples and landed at Srirangam where his maternal uncle stayed. Padmapāda's uncle was a staunch Vaiṣṇava and was not at all happy with the fact that his nephew had accepted saṁnyāsa and adopted the philosophy of Advaita-vedānta, which was, in many ways, contradictory to the philosophy of the Vaiṣṇavas. He, however, concealed his true feelings and appeared to be very hospitable. Padmapāda, in his innocence, shared the commentary with his uncle. The uncle asked Padmapāda to leave the text with him, as he wanted to read it in detail without any hurry. He promised to return the text to Padmapāda when he returned from the pilgrimage. As soon as Padmapāda left Srirangam for resuming his pilgrimage, his uncle burnt away the entire work of Padmapāda because he did not want this work to further strengthen the popularity of Advaita-vedānta. When Padmapāda returned after a few days, the uncle, keeping a sad demeanour, told him that a fire broke out in the house and the work of Padmapāda was burnt away in the process. Though Padmapāda felt sad, he consoled his uncle stating that he remembered each word of the commentary and that he could reproduce it at any time. The uncle felt all his efforts had been in vain. He asked Padmapāda to stay back that night with him. That night, he mixed a specific poison in the dinner that turned Padmapāda into a lunatic the next day. He could not remember anything. The disciple who was accompanying Padmapāda sensed some foul play and immediately decided to take Padmapāda back to the Ācārya.

ADHYĀYA 13

The Dutiful Son

मुक्तामणि त्वं नयनं ममेति राजेति जीवेति चिर सुत त्वम् ।
इत्युक्तवत्यास्तव वाचि मातः ददाम्यहं तण्डुलमेव शुष्कम् ||

Into your mouth, that said 'You are the pearl of my eyes, my prince, may you live long, son!', O Mother! I now offer only dry grains of rice.

—*Mātṛ-pañcakam* verse 1

Meanwhile in Sringeri, one day, Ācārya had a premonition that the end of his mother was close. Hence, he quickly left Sringeri for Kalady along with Citsukha, his childhood friend. On the way, Ācārya discussed with Citsukha the various aspects of Yoga, yogic powers and siddhīs. Soon they reached Kalady and went home, where Āryāmbā was on her deathbed. Her joy knew no bounds as she beheld her dear son Śaṅkara who she was seeing now after nearly sixteen years! Had she not held herself all these years without seeing her beloved son, her only support in life? She had directed all her grief, worries and anxieties into religious and spiritual pursuits. She had realised that the Lord alone is her refuge and had started progressing on the spiritual path guided by the śāstras and the upadeśas she had received from her husband and other elders. These sixteen years she lived a tapasvinī, a renunciate, giving up all her desires, withdrawing all her senses from the sense objects and trying to establish herself in the peace within. When Śaṅkara saw Āryāmbā, he could conspicuously sense the spiritual maturity in her. However, her many years of ritualistic living before had created certain blockages to her attainment of the ultimate realisation. Śaṅkara helped her overcome these by remaining close to her in her last moments and guiding her through the process. Finally, having burnt all her vāsanas and with no desire left within, having annihilated the mind completely, Āryāmbā went into nirvikalpa-samādhi and shed her mortal coil. A strange peace filled the air, which Citsukha could experience profoundly.

Overpowered by the love for Āryāmbā, Ācārya composed five verses (popularly called *Mātṛ-pañcakam*) in praise of his mother and all the mothers of the world. In one of the verses, he says, 'O Mother, at the time of giving me birth, you suffered unbearable pain. But you never complained of all the physical pain and suffering you went through. For even one of those suffering, a son cannot offer atonement.' These, and the rest, would melt the heart of even the cruellest people and move them to tears!

As promised to his mother, Śaṅkara decided to perform her final rites. However, the Nambūdiri community was against a saṁnyāsī performing the final rites of his mother and they threatened to boycott Śaṅkara if he went ahead with the cremation. Śaṅkara paid little heed to them and with the help of a few relatives and Citsukha, cremated his mother in the backyard of the house itself. The family of the relatives who held the legs of the mother came to be called 'Kāl-puḷḷi' or 'Kāppiḷḷi' mana and those who held the mother's head came to be called 'Talai-āṭṭu-puḷḷi' mana. Fast forward years to the 19th century CE, one of the main indicators that helped the thirty-third Jagadguru of Sringeri-maṭha locate the exact location of Śaṅkara's house was that there was a tradition in the locality to light a lamp and pray under an Aśoka tree. The locals believed this to be the place of cremation of Āryāmbā. Āryāmbā also is said to have appeared in dream of the thirty-third Jagadguru and mentioned that she resided under the Aśoka tree! This samādhi of Āryāmbā is now housed within the Śāradā temple in Kalady.

The rest of the disciples joined the Ācārya in a couple of weeks in Kalady. While discussing with them, Citsukha was surprised to know that the other disciples had started from Sringeri immediately after Ācārya and Citsukha but had reached much later. This is when he realised that, while speaking of yogic powers, Ācārya had demonstrated them and accelerated the travel to Kalady! What to say of the greatness of the Ācārya!

This is when the disciple and Padmapāda joined the Ācārya in Kalady. Ācārya and the other disicples were shocked to see the pitiable state of Padmapāda who was laughing and crying like a lunatic. Ācārya took Padmapāda near him and blessed him. With the grace of the Ācārya, Padmapāda's lunacy was cured in a few days' time. Padmapāda fell on the feet of the Ācārya asking for forgiveness for venturing on the pilgrimage despite Ācārya's disapproval. He felt sad that his work was lost, and his memory of the work had also been erased. How could he reproduce the work again? Ācārya consoled him and said that he remembered the work clearly from what he had read of it. Thus, Padmapāda reproduced the work from Ācārya's memory! This is what is available today as *Pañcapādikā*, which is the commentary on the Śaṅkara-bhāṣya for the first four of the *Brahma-sūtra*s (including the *adhyāsa-bhāṣya*).

At this juncture, let us look at what the disciples of Ācārya had to say about him. This is the only external contemporary evidence we have on the Ācārya since all his biographies were written several years after him. In his invocation to the *Pañcapādikā*, Padmapāda says that Ācārya is a rare form of Śiva in the form of a true saṁnyāsī, not interested in any worldly possessions, surrounded by sages, the very form of logic, who is never furious, and a jivan-mukta who has surpassed time.[1] Toṭaka says that Ācārya is Śiva himself[2] bearing the flag of the bull,[3] the most compassionate person,[4] greatest among gurus,[5] expounder of all śāstras and the great Upaniṣads,[6] and the one who gives happiness to all through teaching the path of self-enquiry![7] Sureśvara mentions Ācārya as the one capable of destroying the knots of ignorance,[8] whose rays of glory have pervaded the world like the rays of the full moon,[9] etc. This was the kind of respect, love, adulation and devotion that the Ācārya commanded from his disciples!

The journey of the Ācārya, from the time he left Kalady as a boy of eight, until his return to Kalady at the age of twenty-four, marks his first Bhārata-yātrā. However, much of this time was spent in the study of Vedānta with the guru, writing of the commentaries and establishing the Advaita-siddhānta in the scholarly circles through debates and discussions and the coming together of illustrious disciples. This phase mostly addressed the scholarly class of the society. Most of the society, however, comprised common people, who may not understand the śāstras or have the ability to read and comprehend the scholarly works like the bhāṣyas. True transformation is not possible if this majority is not addressed. It was for this reason that Ācārya decided to undertake his second Bhārata-yātrā, which is popularly referred to as his Digvijaya or spiritual conquest!

ADHYĀYA 14

Digvijaya

तीर्थीकुर्वन्ति तीर्थानि

The greatest of the Bhaktas are the ones who make tīrthas sacred by visiting them!

—*Nārada-bhakti-sūtra* 5.03

Contrary to what we see today, in olden days, temples acted as the religious, cultural, spiritual, educational and administrative hubs of the kingdom. Hence, visiting temples was not just for worship but also to thoroughly understand the social fabric of the society there. Thus, Ācārya's Digvijaya was primarily from one temple to another. The various biographies speak of the Digvijaya with differing sequence of places visited. Hence, what is presented here is a sequence that is geographically more logical. This may or may not corroborate with the biographies. A detailed list of places visited by the Ācārya (based on literary references and traditional accounts) is provided in the appendix (see Śaṅkara's Digvijaya yātrā map with references). A few of these places along with other aspects of the Digvijaya are detailed in this chapter.

Vṛṣabhācala–Guruvayur–Kadampuzha (Kerala)

Ācārya began the Digvijaya from the temple of Vṛṣabhācala in Thrissur, which is closely related to his birth. He then travelled to the temple of Guruvayur – the hub of Vaiṣṇava bhakti in modern Kerala. The vigraha of caturbhuja-nārāyaṇa in this temple is the one that Lord Kṛṣṇa Himself is said to have worshipped in Dwarka. Hence, devotees view the Lord here as the child (called uṇṇi in Malayalam) Kṛṣṇa itself. As per divine will, Ācārya codified the method of worship in the temple as per Kerala-tantra. Guruvayur is among the few temples in Kerala where elaborate Tāntric rituals are performed all through the year without any interruption. During his travels, in a place not very far from Guruvayur, Ācārya noticed a light emanating from deep inside the forest. On approaching the place, Ācārya could experience a divine sanctity. Through his yogic powers he recognised it as the place where Lord Śiva, in his form as Kirāta, had brought forth Ganga by piercing an arrow to the ground to quench the thirst of Pārvatī. Hence, this place came to be called Kāḍan (hunter)–ambu (arrow)–eitha (shot)–puzhā (water stream), which got shortened to Kadampuzha. Ācārya could sense the sanctity of Pārvatī in this place and hence consecrated the power of Devī here.

Chottanikkara (Near Ernakulam in Kerala)

Tradition states that Ācārya wanted to bring to his village Kalady the power of the Goddess that he experienced at Mookambika. This was the temple of Chottanikkara bhagavatī, which is not very far from Kalady. Similar to Mookambika, the Goddess here is worshipped in three forms – as Sarasvatī in the morning, as Lakṣmī in the afternoon and as Durgā in the evening. It is also said that, owing to the love of Śaṅkara, the Goddess accepts the nivedya here before accepting the nivedya at Mookambika! However, it is to be noted that the vigraha at Chottanikkara, contrary to the vigraha at Mookambika, is a svayambhu-sīlā (self-manifested stone) with no definite form. The caturbhuja form of Chottanikkara bhagavatī that we see in images is a covering placed over this stone. This temple is also associated with Vilvamaṅgalam-swamiyar, who comes in the lineage of Śaṅkara.

Tiruchendur (Near Tuticorin in Tamil Nadu)

Ācārya visited Tiruchendur, also known as Jayantipuram, which houses one of the six holy shrines of Lord Subrahmaṇya (called Muruga). This was the place where the Lord camped and vanquished the demon Sūrapadman and his army. It is said that when the Ācārya visited the shrine, he saw a snake going into the sanctum sanctorum to perform worship to the vigraha. This inspired the Ācārya to praise the Lord in the rare bhujaṅga-prayāta metre and composed the *Subrahmaṇya-bhujaṅgam*. In this, Ācārya mentions of the temple resting on a small hillock (called Sugandha-śaila)[1] on the seashore.[2] This temple also has the unique tradition of offering vibhūti (sacred ashes) of the Lord in a pannīr leaf to the devotees. The pannīr leaf has twelve branches in it, representing the twelve hands of the six-faced Ṣaṇmukha (another name for Muruga).

Hence, devotees feel as if the Lord is himself giving the vibhūti with all his twelve hands! Ācārya mentions of this tradition in the stotra.[3] Interestingly, here the worship to the main vigraha is done by the Potti community (from Karnataka) in a Tāntric way (as per Kumāra-tantra), guided by a Tantrī from the Nambūdiri community of Kerala! Probably this was instituted by the Ācārya.

Tiruvidaimarudur (Near Kumbhakonam in Tamil Nadu)

Ācārya visited the temple of Mahāliṅgasvāmi at Tiru-idai-marudur or Madhya-arjunam. This place had been a hub of mīmāṁsakas as also the followers of the Śaiva tradition. Hence, Ācārya faced severe refutation and argumentation on the supremacy of Advaita-vedānta. Even though logically convincing, they were not ready to accept the supremacy of Advaita-vedānta until Śiva himself acknowledged and stated the same! Ācārya is then said to have prayed to the Lord here, and then an arm emerged from the liṅga and stated '*Advaitam-eva-satyam*' (Advaita alone is truth)!

Jambukeshwaram (Near Trichy in Tamil Nadu)

Jambukeśvaram or Tiru-ānai-kāval is a temple in Trichy dedicated to Lord Jambukeśvara (representing the principle of water) and Goddess Akhilāṇḍeśvarī. When Ācārya visited this place, the goddess was in a state of fury owing to the vāmācāra practices being followed here. The people could not even visit the temple. They pleaded to the Ācārya to relieve them of this situation. Ācārya drew all the fury of the

Goddess into two Śrī-cakras designed in the form of earrings (tāṭaṅka) and adorned the same on the ears of the Goddess. He also placed the sanctum of Gaṇeśa right in front of the sanctum of the Goddess so that, when the doors opened at dawn, the first thing she would see would be her dear son. This would also help in containing the fury. The earrings get into a state of disrepair over a period. Even to this day, the Śaṅkarācārya of the Kanchi-maṭha is given the right to repair the earrings and put them back on the Goddess.

Kanchipuram

Kanchipuram has been regarded as one of the foremost cities of Bhārata and a great centre of learning in the south, like Kashi in the north. Hence, the popular phrase 'Nagareṣu Kanchi', i.e., among cities, it is Kanchi. It is also one of the seven mokṣapuris or seats of liberation.[4] Kanchi is a unique congregation of theistic traditions. It is one of the foremost centres of worship for the Śāktas centred around the Kāmākṣī temple, for the Vaiṣṇavas centred around many Divya-deśams including the famous Varadarāja temple, for the Śaivas centred around the Ekāmreśvara temple (one of the foremost of the Śaivite shrines), and for the Kaumāras centred around the Kumara-koṭṭam temple, which has the distinction of having the story of Kumara, i.e., 'Kanda-Purāṇam', composed there by Kacciappa-śivācāriar. Because it was a great centre of learning, scholars from across the country came here to exchange notes and ideas. Thus, we find a strong presence of Buddhist and Jain traditions as well in Kanchi, in addition to the Śaiva, Vaiṣṇava, Śākta, and Kaumāra traditions. Hence, it is impossible to believe that Ācārya, who was on a mission to rejuvenate the Sanātana-dharma and spread the message of the Upaniṣads, would not have visited Kanchi or not stayed here for a good period just like he did in Kashi.

It is a common misconception that it was the Ācārya who consecrated the vigraha of Goddess Kāmākśī. That was not the case. The *kśetra-māhātmya* of Kanchipuram says that the Goddess manifested as Lalitā owing to the prayers of the Devas to put an end to the demon Bhaṇḍāsura. In the battle that ensued, Goddess Lalitā put an end to Bhaṇḍāsura and established herself as Goddess Kāmākśī. Hence, the vigraha of Kāmākśī is svayambhu, i.e., self-manifested. The term Kāmākśī is explained as one who has 'Ka' (indicating Sarasvati) and 'Ma' (indicating Lakṣmī) as her two eyes. The iconography of Kāmākśī is of the Goddess seated in padmāsana, smiling and holding pāsa (noose), ankuśa (goad), sugarcane, and a bunch of flowers in her four hands. Interestingly, this is the form of Goddess Lalitā described in the beginning verses[5] and the dhyāna śloka[6] of the *Lalitā-sahasranāma*. The form of Kāmākśī is the only form that matches this description. Ācārya also praises this form in his *Saundaryalaharī*.[7] Thus, the temple of Kāmākśī has been in existence for ages and has been a great Śākta centre. Furthermore, the pūjā-vidhāna for the Goddess was codified by sage Durvāsā, documented in the text *Saubhāgya-cintāmaṇī*.

When Ācārya came to Kanchi, it is said that the worship of Goddess Kāmākśī had gone into the hands of people following vāmācāra. Due to this, the Goddess had attained a furious form. This started manifesting as famines and droughts in the area. It became impossible for people to visit the temple owing to the fury of the Goddess. The people pleaded with the Ācārya to put an end to these travails. Ācārya argued with these Tāntrics, defeated them in debate and restarted the sāttvic form of worship[8] that was codified by Sage Durvāsā. To contain the fury of the Goddess, he consecrated the Śrī-cakra in front of the Goddess,[9] to which worship is done even to this day.[10] Ācārya stayed in Kanchi for a few days. During this period, he is said to have remodelled the city of Kanchi into Viṣṇu-kanchi around the temple of Lord Varadarāja and Śiva-kanchi around the temple of Lord Ekāmreśa. He also got the Brāhmaṇas to do worship in these temples.[11] We find many sculptures in different temples of Kanchipuram that portray the Ācārya commonly represented as a yati with shaven head and a staff (see Kuppuswami 2013).

Jagannath

Ācārya then visited the famous Puruṣottama kṣetra (Puri) where we have the Nīlācala hillock on which stands the famous Jagannath temple. The place was ruled by the famed King Jajati Kesari of the Somavaṁśī dynasty. However, as in many other temples of the north, Ācārya was shocked to find the dāru-śilā (wooden vigrahas) of Lord Jagannātha, Balabhadra and Subhadrā missing. Instead, worship was being done to sālagrāmas. On enquiry with the elders in the locality, he understood that during invasions, the three vigrahas were put in a huge box and buried in the ground. Another version states that it was kept hidden in big cave near Subarnpur. It remained underground for many years and later when they decided to dig it out, they could not locate it. Ācārya, through his yogic powers, located the spot under a banyan tree near the Chilka lake and asked it to be dug out. Lo! The box was found but the wooden parts of the vigrahas had gotten destroyed. Luckily, the brahma-padārtha (the material that represents the soul of the Lord) was intact. Ācārya, with the help of the king, got the dāru-śilās made again with the brahma-padārtha inside and installed them in the temple. The 'Nava-kalebara' (literally 'new-body') festival was thus celebrated in Puri after nearly a hundred and fifty years. Some accounts state that even the brahma-padārtha had gotten destroyed and a new one had to be created from special sālagrāma stones taken from the Gandaki river with the help of the then king of Nepal. These incidents are recorded in the annals of the Jagannāth temple called *Maṇḍala-pañjī*. This place is also blessed with the presence of śaktī as Vimalā and is one of the fifty-one śaktī pīṭhas. Recognising the spiritual aura of the place, Ācārya decided to establish the Pūrvāmnāya-govardhana-maṭha here with Padmapāda as the first Ācārya.[12] This was also geographically best suited to establish the 'Eastern' maṭha.

Paśupatināth

At the behest of the then king of Nepal, Ācārya travelled to take darśan of Lord Paśupatināth. He was shocked to see that the temple was under the control of people doing occult practices, who had defiled the liṅga and the temple. With the help of the king, these people were driven away and purificatory rituals were done to reinstate the sanctity of the liṅga. Ācārya then ordered for the chief priest (called Bhaṭṭa) to be a Śaiva-trailiṅga-draviḍa-brāhmaṇa with good knowledge of Śaiva-āgama and various other qualifications. The individual was required to be trained by the Sringeri-maṭha. This tradition continues to this day!

Visit to Kailāsa

In some of the versions, it is mentioned that Ācārya travelled to Kailāsa to have the darśana of Lord Śiva and was blessed with five sphaṭika (crystal) liṅgas. These are said to have been placed by the Ācārya in Chidambaram (mokṣa liṅga), Kanchi (yoga liṅga), Sringeri (bhoga liṅga), Nepal (vara liṅga), and Badari or Kedar (mukti liṅga).

Ascending the Sarvajña-pīṭha

It was a practice in those days to have a seat of scholarship in key centres of learning. Sarvajña-pīṭha (seat of omniscience) was one such seat of scholarship and probably among the highest. From various records, we understand that there were multiple sarvajña-pīṭhas across major learning centres of Bhārata, such as Kanchi, Kashmir, etc., as well as in places like Puri. Among these, the one in Kashmir was probably regarded as the highest. The pīṭha is said to have been in the premises of the Śāradā temple situated in the Neelum valley. As mentioned earlier, Śāradā is the deity of Kashmir[13] and hence even the script developed here is called the Śāradā script. The sarvajña-pīṭha here was a pedestal that could be adorned by a person if he or she could satisfactorily clear two rounds of questioning – one by the scholars of Kashmir and the second by the Goddess Śāradā Herself. Such a person would be recognised as a 'Sarvajña'. The sarvajña-pīṭha had four doors, one in each of the four directions,[14] three of which were opened by 'sarvajñas' coming from the northern, eastern and western parts of Bhārata. With the Ācārya clearing the rounds of questioning and being declared a 'sarvajña', the southern door of the pīṭha was opened for the first time. Flanked by all his disciples, Ācārya climbed the stairs of the sarvajña-pīṭha and entered it through the southern door. Amidst sounds of bells, trumpets and horns and people shouting 'Jayati Śaṅkara', Ācārya occupied the sarvajña-pīṭha. What a sight it would have been to behold! Jaya Jaya Śaṅkara! Certain Śaṅkara-vijayas speak of the Ācārya ascending the sarvajña-pīṭha in Kanchi and Puri as well. It is very much possible that the Ācārya must have ascended the sarvajña-pīṭhas in Kashmir, Kanchi and Puri. Are great scholars not given honorary doctorates and made fellows of multiple universities? We could regard this in a similar sense.

The Antardhāna

Ācārya, along with his disciples, then went to Kedar, and after the darśana of the Lord, asked his disciples to not follow him anymore. As they watched, the Ācārya walked up the snowy slopes of the Himalayas and soon disappeared from mortal vision into the misty peaks. The earthly sojourn of the Ācārya had coming to an end with the purpose of his advent completed.

We commonly hear of three versions of the antardhāna of the Ācārya. The most popular is the one described above. The other popular version is that of Ācārya attaining samādhi in Kanchipuram after having spent his last days there. Here, the PSV gives a detailed account of how the Ācārya attained samādhi by merging his gross into the subtle.[15] The third version is that of Ācārya attaining samādhi in the premises of the Vadakkunnathan temple in Thrissur. Even today, there is a place designated as the samādhi of the Ācārya, marked by Vaiṣṇava symbols like the śaṅkha and cakra within the temple premises next to the shrine of the Ācārya.

ADHYĀYA 15

Śaṅkara and the Various Traditions

द्विसप्ततिमतोच्छेत्रे नमः

Prostrations to Him to put an end (and in some cases reformed) the 72 faiths.

—One of the 108 traditional venerations to the Ācārya

As regards the theistic preference of the Ācārya, scholars debate as to whether the Ācārya was a Śaiva or Vaiṣṇava or Śākta! One mahātmā summarised it this way – '*antaḥ śākto bahiḥ śaivaḥ vyavahāre tu vaiṣṇavaḥ*', i.e., Ācārya is Śākta at heart (i.e., has the heart of a mother), outwardly bears all the insignia of a Śaiva like tripuṇḍra (bhasma), rudrākṣa, etc., and has all the qualities of a true Vaiṣṇava! This is what Ācārya was.

Śaṅkara and Śaivism

Most references on Ācārya mention him to be an incarnation of Śiva or one born as an aspect of Śiva[1] or Śiva Himself.[2] They say that Śambhu (another name for Śiva) who was sitting in silence under the tree as Dakṣiṇāmūrti left his silence and started walking on the face of the earth as Śaṅkara.[3] In short, Śiva transformed himself from the grammatical root 'bhū-bhava' (means 'to be') in Śambhu to the root 'kṛ-kara' (means 'to do') in Śaṅkara! Śaṅkara is a name of Rudra as mentioned in the *Rudra-praśna*.[4]

As we have seen earlier, Ācārya was born as a result of worship to Vṛṣācaleśvara in Thrissur; he met his guru on the banks of Narmada in Omkareshwar, propagated the Advaita-siddhānta in Kashi (the land of Viśvanātha), wrote the bhāṣyas in Badari kṣetra, which is said to belong to Lord Kedāreśvara, spent a long time in Srisailam – the sacred mount of Śiva – and finally disappeared into the Kailāsa mountains in Kedar. Thus, we see that all the major milestones in Ācārya's life are related to the major temples of Śiva!

Śaṅkara and Vaiṣṇavism

The Melpāzhūr mana that Āryāmbā belonged to, had temples devoted to Rāma[5] and Kṛṣṇa,[6] both of whom are considered incarnations of Viṣṇu. Also, as mentioned earlier, Śaṅkara, at a very tender age, had reconsecrated the vigraha of Kṛṣṇa in the nearby temple as it was getting eroded due to the change in the flow of the river Pūrṇā.[7] Thus, we see that right from birth, Śaṅkara was growing up in an atmosphere of devotion to Viṣṇu, amongst other deities. It may also be noted that unlike other parts of Tamizhakam (comprising modern-day Tamil Nadu, Kerala and parts of Karnataka and Andhra Pradesh), Malanādu (or modern-day Kerala) always had a healthy co-existence of Śaiva, Vaiṣṇava and other traditions. Hence, one will find the Nambūdiris officiating worship in the Viṣṇu temples wearing tripuṇḍra and not urdhva-tilaka (vertical application of gopī-candana or other materials) or other Vaiṣṇava symbols.

Śaṅkara's deeper understanding of Vaiṣṇavism and devotion to Viṣṇu is reflected in his works. Even in his commentaries on the Prasthāna-trayī, one would not expect to find mention of any theistic aspect. However, we find mentions of Viṣṇu there. In his commentary on *Brahma-sūtra*, to explain the presence of Brahman inside the construct of the physical body, Śaṅkara gives the analogy of the presence of Viṣṇu inside the sālagrāma.[8] In the *Chāndogya-upaniṣad*, to explain the method of doing upāsanā on Brahman by considering (and hence chanting) the names (i.e., the Vedas) itself as Brahman, he gives the analogy of doing upāsanā on Viṣṇu by considering the vigraha itself as Viṣṇu.[9] In the *Bṛhadāraṇyaka-upaniṣad*, to explain the fact that it is impossible to grasp the formless Being through the senses without a symbol like Oṁkāra, he gives the analogy of the need for a vigraha of Viṣṇu to get a vision/understanding of Viṣṇu.[10] In his introduction to the commentary on the Bhagavad Gītā, he glorifies Kṛṣṇa as the incarnation of Viṣṇu, the primeval creator, also known as Nārāyaṇa.[11] Śaṅkara considered Viṣṇu as the Supreme Being itself and not as a part or fraction of it. This is clear from the above examples where he gives the analogy of Viṣṇu while explaining aspects related to Brahman. In many places in his commentaries, he clearly uses Viṣṇu as a synonym for the Supreme Being and Vaiṣṇavam as the state of merging with the Supreme.[12]

Most of the references quoted by the Ācārya in his Prasthāna-traya commentaries are from the Vedas and Upaniṣads itself. Among the few references he gives outside of these is the *Viṣṇu-purāṇa* (three references), which is considered one of the oldest Purāṇas and the foremost of the Vaiṣṇava-purāṇas.

Beyond these, Ācārya's commentary on the *Viṣṇu-sahasranāma* holds a special place, as this gives us insight into Ācārya's understanding and perspective of Vaiṣṇavism. Let us take a deeper look into this commentary of the Ācārya.

The highest number of quotations/references in this commentary come from the *Viṣṇu-purāṇa*, followed by the Bhagavad Gītā. Ācārya begins his commentary by saluting Kṛṣṇa,[13] who is none but the Supreme Self, the same Kṛṣṇa that he speaks of in his Introduction to the Bhagavad Gītā. This salutation bears a lot of resemblance to the starting verse of *Kṛṣṇāṣṭakam*,[14] which is said to have been composed by the young Ācārya, all of eight years, on Lord Kṛṣṇa at Kalady. It is clear from these that the Ācārya considers Kṛṣṇa as the ultimate Brahman that is known by the Vedas and Vedānta, the Supreme Guru and the Supreme witness, and not just as a deity or historical personality.

Coming to the forms of Viṣṇu, Ācārya has praised a number of these in his stotras, such as Jagannātha of Puri, Pāṇḍuraṅga of Pandharpur, Raṅganātha of Srirangam, Lakṣmi-nṛsiṁha, Veṅkateśvara, Rāma, Kṛṣṇa, Acyuta, Govinda and so on. However, the three stotras on Viṣṇu, namely the *Viṣṇu-pādādikeśa*, *Viṣṇu-bhujaṅga* and *Viṣṇu-ṣaṭpadi*, stand apart in Ācārya's immense devotion to Viṣṇu!

In the *Viṣṇu-pādādikeśa*, he praises and worships each aspect of Viṣṇu.

It might be worth noting here that Ācārya had a special bond with the Nṛsiṁha form of Viṣṇu. This is validated by the incident of Nṛsiṁha saving his life from the kāpālika in Srisailam and Ācārya writing a commentary on the *Nṛsiṁha-tāpani-upaniṣad*. This is the only theistic Upaniṣad that Ācārya wrote a commentary on! The upāsanā of Nṛsiṁha continues in many of the traditions of Śaṅkara. For example, we find a close association of the Jagadgurus of the Sringeri-maṭha with Nṛsiṁha upāsanā.

Also, from a Vaiṣṇava perspective, few temples in Bhārata hold very high importance, such as Srirangam, Tirupati, Badari, Puri, etc. Ācārya has been associated with most of these temples, not just from the perspective of visiting the temple and composing a hymn but also reviving the temple and reconsecrating vigrahas, which he did at Badari and Puri.

Śaṅkara and Śāktism

Śāktism, i.e., tradition of worshipping Śaktī as the primeval deity, has been in practice since time immemorial and finds mention in the Vedic literature. From the perspective of śāstras, *Devī-bhāgavata-purāṇa*, *Devī-saptaśatī* (or *Devī-māhātmya*), which is part of the *Mārkaṇḍeya-purāṇa*, *Lalitā-sahasranāma* and *Lalitā-triśatī* (both of which belong to the Lalitopākhyāna section of *Brahmāṇḍa-purāṇa*) are generally considered as the fundamental texts of Śāktism. Of these, the

Ācārya has written a commentary on the *Lalitā-triśatī*. Apart from the various stotras, he composed an independent work called the *Saundaryalaharī*, which encapsulates the essence of devotion to Śaktī. These two texts, in a way, encapsulate Ācārya's views on Śāktism.

Lalitā is considered the highest form of the Goddess in Śāktism, and she is said to be residing along with Śiva in Śrī-nagara,[15] which refers to the Śrī-cakra. Hence the importance of Śrī-cakra in Śākta worship. In the *Saundaryalaharī*, after praising the Goddess, Ācārya defines the Śrī-cakra as a combination of four triangles of Śiva, five triangles of Śaktī, eight and sixteen petals, three circles, and three lines forming a total of forty-four angles.[16] This, along with the fact that he has established the Śrī-cakra in most of the Śaktī temples he visited, proves that Ācārya must have been a great knower and worshipper of the Śrī-cakra, i.e., a Śrī-vidyā-upāsaka. Many of the *Saundaryalaharī* verses closely follow the verses in the *Lalitā-sahasranāma*. For example, the eighth verse[17] of *Saundaryalaharī* speaks of the goddess residing in the middle of the sea of nectar,[18] surrounded by Kadamba trees,[19] in the house made of Cintāmaṇī stones.[20]

A Note on *Tāntric* Worship of Śakti

Tāntric worship of Śaktī can happen through three traditions – Kaula,[21] Miśra and Samaya.[22] The Kaula-mārga primarily uses the pañca-makāra, i.e., madya (alcohol), māṁsa (meat), mudrā (gestures), matsya (fish) and maithuna (sexual contact), either in real (vāma-mārga or left-handed practice) or symbolically (dakṣiṇa-mārga or right-handed practice). On the other hand, Samaya-mārga is completely internal and focused on meditation and the journey towards self-realisation. Miśra is a mix of Kaula and Samaya. Of these, only the Samaya-mārga is Vedic as it has the purpose of self-realisation, while Kaula and Miśra are non-Vedic since their sole objective is the attainment of mundane goals. It is this Samaya-mārga that Ācārya followed and propagated in the Śaktī temples he visited, where he countered with followers of Kaula and Miśra mārgas. The Samaya-mārga is based on Subhāgama tantras, which are five in number – those written by Vasiṣṭha, Sanaka, Śuka, Sanandana and Sanatkumāra. Interestingly, these are also prominent ācāryas of the Advaita-vedānta tradition. The Samaya-mārga has the (Śrī) Cakra-vidyā as the main method of worshipping the Goddess along with various other deities and subsidiary deities of the Śrī-cakra. Śrī-cakra is generally worshipped as a full-meru (three-dimensional pagoda-like structure) or ardha-meru (half of a full meru) or a yantra (meru inscribed on a flat plate).

A Note on Śaṅkara and Tantra

Bhārata is said to have three prominent systems of Tantra – Kashmir system, Gauḍa system (followed in Bengal and the northeast) and Kerala system. While the first two are non-Vedic in nature (i.e., use some aspects of the pañca-makāra), the last one, i.e., Kerala system is Vedic (sāttvic) in nature with the complete absence of pañca-makāra except mudrā, which is a significant part of Kerala-tantra. Tantra is used in

Kerala primarily for worship in temples, be it of Śiva, Viṣṇu, Śaktī, Śāstā or any other deity. A speciality of the Kerala-tantra, as compared to the forms of worship in other parts of the country, is that only the chief priest (called the Tantrī) is allowed to touch the main vigraha in the sanctum sanctorum. The mantras are chanted, mixed with a lot of mudrās but without any sound. While the Tantra tradition in Kerala was primarily handed over in an oral–practical method from generation to generation without any documentation, Ācārya is generally attributed as the first to document the Kerala-tantra through his work *Prapañca-sāra-tantra*, for which Padmapāda is said to have written a commentary (vivaraṇa). Ācārya begins his *Prapañca-sāra-tantra* with an invocation to Śāradā, who is in the form of (three kūṭas of) bījākṣaras (as explained in the *Lalitā-sahasranāma*). Since the Nambūdiris themselves were brought to Kerala by Paraśurāma from other parts of Bhārata, it is possible that Tantra came to Kerala from Kashmir, where Śāradā was worshipped as the primeval deity. In addition, the fact that Ācārya did the consecration of their family deity, Kṛṣṇa, at the age of eight, the consecration of Badari-Nārāyaṇa as per Kerala-tantra at the age of twelve or thirteen, and codified the worship for the Lord in Guruvayur as per the Kerala-tantra amply prove that the Ācārya was an adept in Kerala-tantra.

From where did Ācārya learn tantra? Though we do not find any explicit references of this, it is quite probable that Ācārya learnt it from his father who was also a priest at the nearby Kātyāyanī temple, as also from the experts of tantra in the vicinity.

A Note on the Sects Encountered by Śaṅkara

It is said that, at the time of the Ācārya, there were nearly seventy-two faiths in Bhārata.[23] Many of these had occult and other practices that were threatening the peace of the society and the sustenance of Sanātana-dharma. Ācārya argued with the leaders of many of these faiths and successfully established the Vedic dharma. Some of these faiths got transformed by adopting a Vedic form, some of these got completely extinct, while some continued, albeit in smaller proportions. An obvious doubt in the minds of the readers would be to understand what these seventy-two faiths were. This section is an attempt to enlist these. Each of these has the suffix 'maṭa' which literally means an 'opinion'. Hence, these are different opinions/faiths that had followers behind them. Many of these find mention in the PSV and a few of these in MSV and other biographies. We get more information of some of these faiths from contemporary literature as well, which has analysed faiths and cults that existed in Bhārata in the past (Chattopadhyaya 2000, Nandi 1973).

Below is a list of these seventy-two faiths (to be counted along with the sub-sects mentioned under the main sect). It may be noted that information is not available on all these faiths. Hence, where scanty or no information is available, only the names of the faiths are mentioned.

1. ***Śaiva-mata***: This is the worship of Lord Śiva as the primary deity. Śiva appears as Rudra in the Vedas and then evolving through the Purāṇas and itihāsas into the deity Śiva that is currently seen. The Śaiva mata

encompasses a lot many sub-sects. Some are the ordinary followers of Śiva who worshipped him through the bhakti (devotion) demonstrated in the Purāṇas, Vedic mantras, etc. Some were followers of the Śaiva-siddhānta (mainly in the southern part of the Bhārata) with Śaiva-āgamas as the base, and some with Tāntric influence as well. The others were Pāsupata-Lakulīśas, Kāpālikas, Kālāmukhas, etc. While Śaṅkara greatly opposed the sects that had vāmācāra and non-Vedic practices, he upheld the sāttvic aspect of Śaivism including the ones based on Āgamas. It is only through the Śaiva-āgamas, that he was able to reconsecrate/restart the worship in temples like Paśupatināth in Nepal. PSV (Chapter 4) speaks of Śaṅkara encountering six types of Śaivas in Rameshwaram.

a. ***Śaivas***: who bore the symbol of liṅga on their hands.
b. ***Raudras***: who bore the symbol of trisula (trident) on their foreheads.
c. ***Ugras***: who bore the symbol of ḍamaruka (drum) on their hands.
d. ***Bhaktas***: who bore the symbol of liṅga on their foreheads.
e. ***Jaṅgamas***: who bore the symbol of triśūla in their heart and carried a stone liṅga on their heads.
f. ***Pāsupatas***: who bore the symbol of liṅga on their forehead, hands, heart, and navel. Pāsupata–lakulīśa–mata was a tradition of Śiva as Pāsupati, which was propagated by Lakulīśa where Pāsupati was the primeval deity. Lakulīśa was considered an incarnation of Śiva and is always depicted nude. Their tenets seem

very similar to the ones mentioned under Māheśvaras. Ācārya encountered Nīlakaṇṭha, the leader of the Pāsupata-mata, and his student Haradatta in Gokarna. Nīlakaṇṭha was a revered master of Śaivism and had commented on the Vedānta *Brahma-sūtras* in the light of Pāsupata-mata, which was called *Śiva-tatpara-sūtra-bhāṣya.*[24]

2. ***Caṇḍa-bhairava mata***: Followers of this faith had liṅga symbols etched on their foreheads, smeared with white ash all over the body, wearing garlands of rudrākṣa on the head, neck and hands. Ācārya met one of the leaders of this faith called Padmabhāskara.

3. ***Māheśvara-mata***: In his work *Bhāmatī*, Vācaspati Miśra, who came very soon after the Ācārya, explains that Māheśvaras had four sub-sects – Śaivas, Pāsupata, Kāruṇikasiddhāntins, and Kāpālikas. The tenets for all these four sects were laid down by Maheśvara himself. These are (1) the efficient cause is Īśvara (2) the effect or material cause is pradhāna (3) yoga includes various practices such as dhyāna, dhāraṇā, etc. (4) vidhi includes various rituals to be performed, and finally (5) dukhānta, i.e., cessation of sorrow is mokṣa or liberation.[25] Śaṅkara considers them a worthy opponent because of their sāttvic nature and refutes their theory that Lord can only be an efficient cause[26] given the Upaniṣadic dictum that Brahman is both the material and efficient cause.

   a. ***Kāpālika-mata:*** This is the worship of Kapālī (form of Śiva holding the skull) and Bhairava (the chief attendant of Śiva). This sect had a large share of vāmācāra and non-Vedic practices including human sacrifice. As we have seen earlier, Śaṅkara was about to be beheaded by Ugra-bhairava, a fierce Kāpālika, during his stay at Srisailam. Śaṅkara also encountered Krakaca-bhairava in Karnataka. MSV states that Krakaca had ashes from the cremation ground smeared all over his body and in his hands were a skull and a trident. These were the emblems of this cult. A sub-sect of this faith had people such as Unmatta-bhairava who, in addition, wore a garland of skulls and had painted ink on their forehead. Kālāmukhas is another sect of Śaivas, sometimes used interchangeably with Kāpālikas and sometimes distinguished (Lorenzen 1991).

4. ***Vīra-śaiva-mata***: This is a form of Śiva worship based on the āgamas that developed and flourished more in the Karnataka region. This is also referred to as the Liṅgāyat tradition. MSV mentions of this tradition.[27]
5. ***Mallāri-mata***: This is the worship of Mallāri, the folk deity who is popularly called Khāṇḍobā and is considered a manifestation of Śiva. He is also called Mārtāṇḍa-bhairava. This tradition is predominant in the Deccan regions, i.e., modern-day Maharashtra, Karnataka and Andhra Pradesh. In the Mallari temple, devotees behave like dogs in every respect, barking and eating off the ground (Zoller 2017). It is said Mallāri had transformed tigers into humans and asked them to behave like dogs! Ācārya met the followers of this cult in Anumalla.

6. *Vaiṣṇava-mata*: This essentially means the worship of Lord Viṣṇu. In the *Ṛgveda*, Viṣṇu is a minor diety who is the brother of Indra (called Upendra). In the Brāhmaṇa literature, Viṣṇu occupied a more important position as the foremost of deities[28] and protector of yajñas. In later times, this cult absorbed other sects such as Vāsudevaka, Bhāgavata, Sātvata, Aikāntika, Pāñcarātrika, etc., which worshipped various deities such as Vāsudeva, Kṛṣṇa, Rāma, Nṛsiṁha, Nārāyaṇa, etc. Most Vaiṣṇava sect followers were seen to have various symbols of Vaiṣṇavism on their body. While Vaiṣṇavism was hugely prevalent in the early ages mainly in the north, later it travelled south with the Guptas and became a predominant tradition in the south of the Vindhyas. This, later, led to the emergence of Vaiṣṇava-bhakti saints, the Āzhvārs, who heralded the beginning of Bhakti movement in Bhārata. PSV mentions of Ācārya encountering six types of Vaiṣṇavas at Anantaśayanam (modern-day Thiruvananthapuram). These are (1) Bhaktas that had two categories – jñāna bhaktas and karma bhaktas (2) Bhāgavata (3) Vaiṣṇava (4) Pāñcarātra (5) Vaikhānasa and (6) Karma-hīna-Vaiṣṇava.

   a. ***(Vaiṣṇava) jñāna bhakta-mata*** who believed in the jñāna mārga like Viṣṇu śarmā.
   b. ***(Vaiṣṇava) karma bhakta-mata*** who believed in the karma mārga like Brahmagupta.
   c. ***Bhāgavata-mata:*** This was the worship of Vāsudeva-Viṣṇu with 'Oṁ namo bhagavata vāsudevāya' being the mūla mantra. This was primarily propagated

during the Gupta period who called themselves as 'Parama-bhāgavatas'. Later, the sect identified Kṛṣṇa with Vāsudeva-Viṣṇu.

d. *Vaiṣṇava mata*: They were followers of Viṣṇu who believed that going to Vaikuṇṭha required the individuals to have symbols of śaṅkha, cakra, etc., on the body. Such individuals who bear the Nārāyaṇa mudra and chant the eight-syllabled mantra go to Vaikuṇṭha. Ācārya met one of the leaders of this faith called Śārṅgapāṇi.

e. *Pāñcarātra-mata*: Originally this was based on Pāñcarātra rite of the Vedas that is said to have been expounded by Sage Nārāyaṇa. Later, it seems to have been transformed into the worship of the catur-vyūha form of Viṣṇu as Vāsudeva (Kṛṣṇa), Saṅkarṣaṇa (Balarāma), Pradyumna (Son of Kṛṣṇa and Rukmiṇī), and Aniruddha (Son of Pradyumna and Rukmavatī). Later, certain Śākta Tāntric principles also seem to have got introduced into this tradition. Today, the Pāñcarātra tradition is one of the two major traditions of Vaiṣṇavism (the other being Vaikhānasa) as regards to temple worship and rituals. The temples that follow Pāñcarātra sampradaya include the Srirangam and Varadaraja temples in Kanchipuram. Rāmānuja belonged to the Pāñcarātra sampradaya. Pañca (five) saṁskāras is an important aspect of this tradition, one of which is to have imprints of śaṅkha and cakra on the arms.

f. *Vaikhānasa-mata*: As mentioned above, this is one of the two major traditions of Vaiṣṇaviṣm (the other being Pāñcarātra) as regards to temple worship and rituals. It is said to have come down from sage Vikhānasa. The temples that follow Vaikhānasa sampradaya include the Tirumala Tirupati and Triplicane Pārthasārathi temples. Ācārya met one of the leaders of this faith called Vyāsadāsa.

g. *Karma-hīna-Vaiṣṇava-mata*: This is the worship of Viṣṇu without performing any rituals or actions. They believe that surrendering to Viṣṇu is the only thing to be done and other duties including prescribed duties need not be performed. Ācārya is said to have encountered them in Srirangam.

7. *Gopāla-kṛṣṇa-mata*: These were worshippers of the child Kṛṣṇa who grew in the house of Nanda along with his brother Balarāma. They, thus, worshipped only two of the catur-vyūhas of the Pāñcarātras, i.e., Vāsudeva (Kṛṣṇa) and Saṅkarṣaṇa (Balarāma). This sect was prevalent in Mathura, Vrindavan, Bengal and Jodhpur. Especially in Bengal, the sect started imbibing vāmācara aspects of Tantra centred on the amorous plays of Kṛṣṇa with the gopīs.

8. *Viṣvaksena-mata*: This is the worship of Viṣvaksena, the commander-in-chief of Viṣṇu, as the primeval deity. The followers believed that by worshipping Viṣvaksena, they would reach Vaikuṇṭha. They wore symbols of śaṅkha, cakra, etc., and carried staffs in their arms.

9. *(Ādi) Varāha-mata:* This is the worship of Lord Ādi Varāha (Viṣṇu in the form of a wild boar) as the primeval deity. Followers of this faith had symbols of the moon or the teeth of Varāha painted on their hands.
10. ***Śeṣa-mata***: These were people who believed that being dressed as Śeṣa, the serpent-bed of Viṣṇu, they would attain liberation, since Śeṣa is extremely close to Viṣṇu's heart!
11. *Garuḍa-mata*: These were people who believed that by worshipping Garuḍa, the eagle-vehicle of Viṣṇu, they would attain liberation, since Garuḍa is extremely close to Viṣṇu's heart!
12. ***Śaktī -mata:*** This is the worship of Śaktī as the central deity. PSV mentions of Ācārya meeting the Śāktas in Bhavānīpura, which probably corresponds to modern-day Tulajapur, one of the fifty-one Śaktī pīṭhas, where we see the famous Tulajā Bhavānī temple.
13. *Mahā-lakṣmī-mata:* This is the worship of Goddess Lakṣmī as the primeval deity, where followers wore garlands of lotus, had symbols of lotus imprinted on the body and wore vermillion on the forehead. PSV mentions of Ācārya meeting the followers of this sect from Kuvalayapura, which probably corresponds to modern-day Kolhapur where we see the famous Mahalakṣmī temple.
14. ***Śāradā-mata:*** This is the worship of Goddess Sarasvatī as the primeval deity, where the followers bore symbols of book, lotus, etc., on their bodies. Ācārya met leaders

of this faith such as Nigama, Sāvitra, Parāgama, Suvāk, Avyakta, Sarva-vāk, etc.

15. *Rāja-śyāmalā-mata:* This is the worship of Goddess Rāja-śyāmalā, also referred to as Mātaṅgī, who is one of the ten forms of Śaktī (Daśa-mahā-vidyā). They worship the Goddess through vāmācāra. Ācārya met leaders of this faith such as Śaktivilāsa, Cidānanda, etc.

16. *Saura-mata:* This is the worship of Lord Sūrya or Sun as the primary deity. While worship of the Sun is prevalent across Vedic traditions, here it refers to an exclusive worship of the Sun by using marks of red sandal paste, wearing garlands of red flowers and repeating the eight-syllabled mantra of Sūrya.[29] PSV speaks of Ācārya meeting a Saura leader called Divākara. Therein are also mentioned six forms of Saura traditions:

    a. Worshippers of the rising sun as the Supreme deity responsible for creation
    b. Worshippers of the setting sun as the Supreme deity responsible for dissolution
    c. Worshippers of the setting sun as the Supreme deity responsible for sustenance
    d. Worshippers of Sun in all three forms and as representative of all duties. They visualise the Supreme with golden moustache, golden hair, etc.
    e. Extremely focused worshippers who will not even have an iota of food without a view of the Sun. They worship the Sun with the sixteen upacāras and surrender all their actions to Him.

f. Worshippers with symbol of the orb marked on their forehead, arms and chest, which seemed to be Tāntric in nature (Chattopadhyaya 2000).

17. *Gaṇapati-mata*: This is the worship of Lord Gaṇapati as the primeval deity. Gaṇapati finds mention as Brahmaṇaspati in the *Ṛgveda*. He is the lord of the gaṇas and lord of intelligence. The form of Gaṇapati we know today developed more in the itihāsas and Purāṇas. Gaṇapati is generally considered as one of the parivāra-devatas and hence we find a sanctum for Gaṇapati in temples of all other deities. However, Gāṇapatya is the tradition of worshipping Gaṇapati as the sole, primeval deity. Ācārya is said to have met the followers of this tradition at a place called Gaṇavaram, which should have been a place between modern-day Maharashtra and Karnataka as these were the states that became the hubs of Gāṇapatya worship in later times. There were six sub-sects of this faith.

   a. ***Mahā-gaṇapati-mata***: This is the worship of Mahā-gaṇapati as the primeval deity. Ācārya met the leader of this faith called Girijāputra.

   b. ***Haridrā-gaṇapati-mata***: This is the worship of Haridrā-gaṇapati as the primeval deity.

   c. ***Ucchiṣṭa-gaṇapati-mata***: This is the worship of Ucchiṣṭa-gaṇapati as the primeval deity. This is a Tāntric form of worship. Ācārya met the leader of this faith called Herambasuta.

   d. ***Navanīta-gaṇapati-mata***: This is the worship of Navanīta-gaṇapati as the primeval deity.

e. *Svarṇa-gaṇapati-mata*: This is the worship of Svarṇa-gaṇapati as the primeval deity.

f. *Santāna-gaṇapati-mata*: This is the worship of Santāna-gaṇapati as the primeval deity.

18. *Kaumāra/Kārtikeya-mata*: This mata is centred on the worship of Lord Subrahmaṇya called variedly as Kumāra, Kārtikeya, Skanda, etc. He was the deity of war and had significant following among the Guptas. The ancient city of Rohitaka (modern-day Rohtak) is said to have been associated with Kaumāra/Kārtikeya. The cult of Murugan/Ceyyōn was a prominent cult in the Tamizh land where Murugan was considered the lord of the hilly regions (kuriñji) and is mentioned as a lord worshipped by the tribal people and the foremost Brāhmaṇas alike. We find a lot of references to this in the Tiru-murugātṛuppaḍai of the Tamizh poet Nakkīrar. Though we do not find explicit references to followers of this faith in the biographies of Ācārya, he should have encountered some devotees of this tradition during his visits to temples of Kukke Subrahmaṇya and Tiruchendur.

19. *Agni-vādi-mata*: This is the worship of agni or fire as the primary deity. Again, while the worship of agni is central to all Vedic rituals, this tradition believes in the supremacy of agni over all other deities and as the one responsible for the creation, sustenance and destruction of the world. PSV mentions names like Suhotras, Vītihotras and Kavyavāhanas, who either were leaders of this faith or sub-sects of this faith.

20. *Hiraṇyagarbha-mata*: This is the worship of Hiraṇyagarbha (earliest manifest form of Brahman as per Vedānta; in some cases, also refers to Brahmā, the creator) as the supreme deity. PSV (Chapter 11) mentions of Ācārya encountering the followers at Subrahmaṇya kṣetra in Kukke.
21. *Kṣapaṇaka-mata*: PSV mentions of these as followers of Kāla or time as the supreme deity. They wore the loincloth and carried various astronomical instruments with them. In few other references, Kṣapaṇaka is the term associated with Digambara Jainas.
22. *Manmatha-mata*: Centred on the worship of Manmatha or Kāmadeva (the lord of love) as the primary deity. Ācārya met the followers of this cult in Varutapuri, who bore the symbol of Manmatha, i.e., the flowery bow, on their hands.
23. *Kubera-mata*: Centred on the worship of Kubera (the lord of wealth and the king of yakṣas) as the primary deity. Ācārya met the followers of this faith, who were wearing garlands of gold and gems, in a place called Yakṣālaya in Māgadha.
24. *Indra-mata*: Centred on the worship of Indra (the lord of the celestials) as the primary deity. We find references to this in the *Śrīmad-bhāgavata*. The tribe of Nanda in Gokula had an annual worship for Indra, which was discontinued by Kṛṣṇa.
25. *Yama-mata*: Centred on the worship of Yama (the lord of death) as the primary deity. The followers dressed up as a buffalo (the vehicle of Yama) and painted their hands red.

26. *Varuṇa-mata*: Centred on the worship of Varuṇa (the lord of waters) as the primary deity. The followers bore symbol of Varuṇa, i.e., 'pāśa' or noose, on their bodies.
27. *Vāyu-mata*: Centred on the worship of Vāyu (the lord of wind) as the primary deity. The followers bore symbol of Vāyu, i.e., dhvaja or flag, on their bodies.
28. *Bhūmi-mata*: Centred on the worship of the earth as the primary deity. The followers bore symbol of Bhūmi, i.e., a circle, on their bodies.
29. *Udaka-mata*: Centred on the worship of the water as the primary deity. The followers bore symbol of water, i.e., a bindu or drop, on their bodies.
30. *Śūnya-mata*: Centred on the belief that 'Nothingness' is Supreme.
31. *Loka-mata*: Centred on the worship of the fourteen worlds[30] as Supreme.
32. *Guṇa-mata*: Centred on the belief that qualities or attributes are the Supreme.
33. *Sāṅkhya-mata*: This was centred on the sāṅkhya darśana of Maharṣi Kapila who believe that Pradhāna or Prakṛti is the Supreme and the cause of the Universe.
34. *Yoga (or Pātañjala)-mata*: This is centred on the Yoga darśana of Maharṣi Pātañjali.
35. *Pīluvādi-mata*: This is centred on the nyāya-vaiśeṣika darśanas of Maharṣi Gautama and Maharṣi Kaṇāda. The term 'pīlu' refers to paramāṇu (sub-atomic particles) and this faith refers to the pre-Praśastapāda Vaiśeṣikas who were followers of Kaṇāda who believed that the paramāṇus are the independent entities of the Universe.

Ācārya met leaders of this faith such as Śiva-bhaṭṭa and Śiva-gaṅga-nātha.

36. *Karma-mata*: This is centred on the performance of prescribed rituals itself as the means for liberation. This should be referring to pūrva-mīmāṁsā that Ācārya had as the main opponent (pradhāna malla) in most of his śāstric works.
37. *Candra-mata*: Centred on the worship of Candra-graha (Moon) as the primary deity. Ācārya met the leader of this faith called Śivābharaṇa.
38. *Bhauma-mata*: Centred on the worship of Kuja or Maṅgala-graha (Mars) as the primary deity.
39. *Budha-mata*: Centred on the worship of Budha-graha (Mercury) as the primary deity.
40. *Bṛhaspati-mata*: Centred on the worship of Guru-graha (Jupiter) as the primary deity.
41. *Śukra-mata*: Centred on the worship of śukra-graha (Venus) as the primary deity.
42. *Śanaiścara-mata*: Centred on the worship of Śani-graha (Saturn) as the primary deity.
43. *Rāhu-mata*: Centred on the worship of Rāhu-ketu-graha as the primary deity.
44. *Pitṛ-mata*: Centred on the worship of manes with pitṛ karma being the most important.
45. *Siddha-mata*: These were worshippers of the siddhis (mystical powers) that one obtains through various practices and the words of the siddhas. These include winning over the five elements, able to transmigrate from one body to another (para-kāya-praveśana), growing the

body large and making it minute, becoming invisible, etc. They believed that knowing this is the ultimate purpose of life. Ācārya explained them the futility of these stating that these were slaves to a knower of Brahman. Ācārya met followers of this faith such as Cira-kīrtị, Nityānanda, Parārjuna, etc.

46. *Gandharva-mata*: This was the worship of Gandharva-rājā Viśvavasū through the art of music. They believed that this worship itself would give the ultimate bliss of Brahman. Ācārya clarified that Vedas do not attest this and that Brahman is beyond all these.

47. *Bhūta-vetāla-mata*: This was the worship centred on spirits, ghosts and goblins.

48. *Cārvāka-mata*: This is the materialistic school also called as Lokāyata-mata or Bārhaspatya-mata. It is one of the three popular nāstika-darśanas or heterodox schools of philosophy. It is a school that accepts only direct perception as a valid source of knowledge, i.e., what I see and perceive is what I believe.

49. *Arhata (Jaina)-mata*: This is the worship and followership of the twenty-four tīrthaṅkaras starting with Ṛṣabha deva and ending with Mahāvīrā. This cult arose primarily to oppose certain aspects of Vedic ritualism and propagate the aspects of truth, non-violence, non-stealing, non-hoarding and continence. It has two traditions of ascetism - Digaṁbara (nude ascetics) and Śvetāṁbara (white-clothed ascetics). Ācārya seems to have encountered the Jainas (referred

to as Arhatas) in the Bāhlika deśa (mostly identified with modern-day Balkh in Afghanistan).[31]

50. ***Bauddha-mata***: This is the following that developed around the teachings of Gautama Buddha, popularly called Buddhism. This, along with Jaina mata, developed as a response to the extreme ritualism of the Vedas, which at some point had overshadowed the Upaniṣadic teachings. However, it focused only on the practice of basic qualities such as truth, non-violence, non-stealing, non-hoarding and continence without providing enough anchorage to the society through action-oriented work.
51. ***Saugata-mata***: PSV mentions of Saugatas as followers of the dictum that life is about enjoyment and there is nothing called rebirth. Hence, one needs to be well fed, which is indicative of the happiness one is enjoying and that alone is bliss. These seem similar to the Cārvāka-mata. It may also be noted that in many references, Bauddhas are mentioned as Saugatas.

ADHYĀYA 16

Śaṅkara and Yoga

ब्रह्मरन्ध्रगते वायौ गिरेः प्रस्रवणं भवेत् |
शृणोति श्रवणातीतं नादं मुक्तिर्नसंशयः ||

When the prana becomes stable at the brahma-randhra,
consciousness flows like the flow from the top of a mountain.
One hears the anahata-sound, which is beyond the range of
hearing, and there is no doubt that one gets mukti.

—*Yoga-tārāvali* verse 29

The term 'yoga' can be understood in two ways – yoga as a system of philosophy (called yoga-darśana) and yoga as a science (called yoga-śāstra). Yoga-śāstra, which is based on the *Yoga-sūtras* of Patañjali, has the cessation of modifications of the mind-stuff[1] and the subsequent establishment of the individual in his/her 'true self'[2] as its sole objective. This is very close to Vedānta śāstra that focuses on the inward journey of the individual, wherein the yoga-śāstra offers all the necessary tools and instruments needed for the inward journey. Yoga-darśana on the other hand, being a system of philosophy, needs to have a worldview as well, which it draws heavily from sāṅkhya darśana, because there is almost nothing to speak on this from the *yoga-sutras*. Understanding this difference is important because while Śaṅkara refutes various aspects of sāṅkhya-darśana, and hence yoga-darśana as well, in his commentaries, he clearly accepts the aspects of yoga-śāstra, which are integral to Vedānta. This is very evident in his commentary on the *Brahma-sūtra* (2.1.3), which deals with this topic in detail. Herein, Śaṅkara clearly states that with the refutation of the sāṅkhya philosophy, the yoga philosophy is also refuted.[3] However, there are aspects of yoga (such as the aṣṭāṅga-yoga or eight-limbed yoga)[4] which are part of the yoga-śāstra, and which find mention in the Upaniṣads itself. Hence, these cannot be ignored and do form an essential part of the Vedānta-śāstra.

From the earlier chapters, it is amply clear that Śaṅkara was highly knowledgeable on yoga-śāstra and an adept practitioner of the same. He was a great yogī himself. Śaṅkara's views on yoga and his expertise in it were known from two sources – his works and his biographies. Let us take a closer look at these. It may be noted that the term yoga or yogī used in this chapter refers to the yoga-śāstra and not the yoga-darśana.

Yoga in Śaṅkara's Works

As far as the references in the Prasthāna-traya-bhāṣya are concerned, Śaṅkara quotes the yoga-sūtras related to the five modifications of the mind in his *Brahma-sūtra-bhāṣya*.[5] He speaks of the yogī taking up various bodies through the power of yoga.[6] He refers to the āsanas mentioned in the yoga-sūtras[7] and speaks of the suṣumna nāḍi above the hṛdaya,[8] also mentioned in the yoga-sutras. In his *Viṣṇu-sahasranāma-bhāṣya*, Śaṅkara defines yoga as the feeling of oneness attained with the Supreme Being through the control of the mind along with organs of knowledge.[9]

Beyond the references in the bhāṣyas, Śaṅkara has composed one work on yoga known as *Yoga-tārāvali*. This is primarily a work on Haṭhayoga. *Gheraṇḍa-samhitā*, *Śiva-samhitā* and *Haṭhayoga-pradīpikā* are considered the three canonical texts of classical Haṭhayoga. All these texts are variedly dated between the 15th–17th century CE. Even the early texts on Haṭhayoga are dated to 10th–11th century CE. Given this, *Yoga-tārāvali* inevitably becomes one of the earliest works on Haṭhayoga, whichever version of the date of Śaṅkara one considers. Also, Śaṅkara says at one place that Haṭha speaks of various kumbhakas, of which kevala-kumbhaka is the best.[10] This is evidence enough to say that Śaṅkara had probably read most of the Haṭhayoga śāstras extant during his time, which is even before the time of the early Haṭhayoga texts.

We can see the influence of *Yoga-tārāvali* on the texts of Haṭhayoga. In the second and fourth verses of *Yoga-tārāvali*, Śaṅkara speaks of the importance of meditation on sound. The interesting fact here is that the second verse of *Yoga-tārāvali*[11] and the sixty-sixth verse of *Haṭhayoga-pradīpikā*[12] are very similar even in their construction! In verse five, Śaṅkara explains the importance of the three bandhas (Oḍḍyāṇa, Mūla and Jālandhara), which are among the three most powerful bandhas or locks in Haṭhayoga. He also speaks of manonmani (the mindless state), kevala-kumbhaka, raja-yoga, etc., in the subsequent verses detailed in the Haṭhayoga texts.

Śaṅkara: The Yogī

From the biographies of the Ācārya, we get a few references of how great an expert he was in the practice of yoga. MSV mentions of one such stance when at Srisailam, a kāpālika came to request for Ācārya's head to be offered to his deity Bhairava. As narrated earlier, Ācārya obliged and suggested that he will get into nirvikalpa-samādhi and then the kāpālika could behead him without any issue. MSV (11.29) says that Ācārya uttered the syllable 'Om' and withdrew the senses into the mind and mind into the self, going into nirvikalpa-samādhi. His posture in samādhi is described as steady neck and backbone, palms lying supine on the knees, calm face, half-open eyes fixed on the tip of the nose. This probably refers to the manonmani state and laya attained through nāda that the *Haṭhayoga-pradīpikā* mentions.[13] This could also refer to the amanaska-mudrā[14] that Ācārya speaks in the *Yoga-tārāvali*. Interestingly, the composition of *Yoga-tārāvali* is generally attributed to his stay at Srisailam as he mentions Srisailam as a highly powerful place to attain perfection in the ultimate of Yoga i.e., samādhi.[15]

ADHYĀYA 17

The Tradition of Śaṅkara

सदाशिव समारम्भां शङ्कराचार्य मध्यमां अस्मदाचार्य पर्यन्तां वन्दे गुरु परम्पराम् |

I prostrate before the guru-paramparā that began with Sadāśiva followed by (great masters reaching up to) Śaṅkara (in the middle) and continues till date upto the current Ācārya!

—Advaita guru-paramparā stotra

The entire Vedic tradition is based on sampradāya or paramparā, which is the unbroken transmission of knowledge from one generation to the other in the prescribed way. As this transmission mostly happened from a teacher to a student, this is commonly referred to as the guru-śiṣya-paramparā or simply guru-paramparā. Vedānta-śāstra being the ultimate essence of the Vedas has come down to us across generations through many such branches of tradition. Speaking of the Advaita-vedānta guru-paramparā, given below is the well-accepted lineage until Śaṅkara.

नारायणः → पद्मभवः (ब्रह्मा) → वसिष्ठः → शक्तिः → पराशरः →
व्यासः → शुकः → गौडपादः → गोविन्दः (गोविन्द भगवत्पादाः) →
शङ्करः (शङ्कर भगवत्पादाः)

Coming to the tradition of Śaṅkara, we commonly speak of his four primary disciples – Padmapāda, Sureśvara, Hastāmalaka and Toṭaka. We understand the lineage of Śaṅkara today mainly through the four 'Āmnāya-maṭhas' established in the four corners of Bhārata and headed by these primary disciples. These are Paścimāmnāya or Western maṭha, also called Śāradā maṭha in Dwarka; Pūrvāmnāya or Eastern maṭha, also called Govardhana maṭha in Puri; Uttarāmnāya or Northern maṭha, also called Jyotirmaṭha or Joshimaṭha in Badarinath; and Dakṣiṇāmnāya or Southern maṭha, also called Sringeri-maṭha in Sringeri. However, these comprise but a part of the tradition of Śaṅkara. Apart from the primary stream of guru–śiṣyas we have in the 'Āmnāya-maṭhas', the heads of these maṭhas have at various points of time initiated qualified aspirants into saṁnyāsa. Some of these initiated aspirants have established their own maṭhas as well. Also, the Śaṅkara-vijayas speak of many more disciples (in addition to the four mentioned above) who were with the Ācārya. For example, PSV speaks of Samitpāṇi, Cidvilāsa, Jñānakanda, Viṣṇugupta, Śuddhakīrti, Bhānu, Marīci, Kṛṣṇadarśana, Buddhi-vṛddhi, Viriñcipāda, Śuddhānanta and Ānandagiri. Many of them had lineages of śiṣyas, some of which are still extant. There, of course, exists the challenge to verify the authenticity of these lineages, as many of them may not have documented evidence.

Given this context, the author would like to visualise the Śaṅkara sampradāya as a huge tree, with Śaṅkara representing the trunk, the roots as his predecessors, the main branches of the tree as the Āmnāya-maṭhas and the other traditions as the sub-branches! Most of the sub-branches have emerged from the main branches. However, each branch (be it main or subsidiary) is a part of the tree and has the capability to bear leaves, flowers and fruits as much as the others. Just a few branches withering away does not affect the tree, as the roots and the trunk are still strong, being nourished by the light of Brahman, the water of guru-bhaktī on the soil of Vedānta!

In our Sanātana-dharma, saṁnyāsa is an essential stage of life every individual must get into, either after completing all their responsibilities, or even earlier depending on their spiritual maturity.[1] We have ample references to saṁnyāsīs and even different categories of them in our śāstras. However, we do not see a tradition of institutionalising saṁnyāsa. In fact, the saṁnyāsī is the one who has renounced all relations and bondages and is expected to be peripatetic, not staying in one place for too long. Śaṅkara himself emphasises these in his commentaries, drawing references from various śāstras. Then why did Śaṅkara establish maṭhas?

Some of the reasons could be the following –

- The tradition of establishing a maṭha or a monastery seems to have come into vogue from the time of the Buddha (in the form of saṅgha) and seems to have followed suit during the time of Śaṅkara. Because the Vedic dharma had to be revived and the others (in this case Bauddhas and Jainas) seemed to have organised themselves very well in an institutional way, Śaṅkara would have felt the need to do the same to counter this. During the time of Śaṅkara, the social stature of the saṁnyāsī also seems to have come down, especially within Sanātana-dharma, given the ill practices of the Buddha and Jaina bhikṣus and their role in degrading the Vedic dharma. We find evidence of this in the episode of Śaṅkara meeting Maṇḍana Miṣra, when the latter is said to have looked at Śaṅkara with disdain because he was a saṁnyāsī!

- Śaṅkara could have foreseen the future where many such organised and institutional factions could emerge and challenge the existence of Vedic dharma. Hence, he probably felt the need to establish these maṭhas as centres to safeguard, uphold and propagate the Sanātana-dharma among the people.

Whatever be the case, the maṭhas have been doing yeomen service in disseminating the message of the Vedas and Upaniṣads among the people not just in Bhārata but also across the globe.

Daśanāmī System

Now coming to the order of saṁnyāsīs, we find six categories mentioned in the Upaniṣads – Kuṭīcaka, Bahūdaka, Haṁsa, Paramahaṁsa, Turīyātīta and Avadhūta.[2] Śaṅkara introduced what we call the Daśanāmī system (literally deca-nomenclatured system) by which the saṁnyāsīs initiated by the Ācārya and his disciples were given one of the ten titles of the Daśanāmī system. These ten titles are Tīrtha, Āśrama, Vana, Araṇya, Giri, Parvata, Sāgara, Sarasvati, Bhārati and Puri. This has been one of the important aspects in establishing that a particular saṁnyāsī or tradition with an initiated name ending in any one of these ten titles of the Daśanāmī system belongs to the Śaṅkara Sampradāya. These titles are tied back to the Āmnāya-maṭhas, where a saṁnyāsī initiated by a particular Āmnāya-maṭha is initiated with a name ending in one of the titles associated with that particular maṭha. The table given below, sourced from the *Maṭhāmnāya*, gives this association.

Name as per Daśanāmī system	Associated Āmnāya-maṭha
Tīrtha	Paścimāmnāya-maṭha (Dwarka)
Āśrama	Paścimāmnāya-maṭha (Dwarka)
Vana	Pūrvāmnāya-maṭha (Puri)
Araṇya	Pūrvāmnāya-maṭha (Puri)
Giri	Uttarāmnāya-maṭha (Badarinath)
Parvata	Uttarāmnāya-maṭha (Badarinath)
Sāgara	Uttarāmnāya-maṭha (Badarinath)
Sarasvati (or Saraswati)	Dakṣiṇāmnāya-maṭha (Sringeri)
Bhārati	Dakṣiṇāmnāya-maṭha (Sringeri)
Puri	Dakṣiṇāmnāya-maṭha (Sringeri)

Some observations

When we look at the detailed records of the pontiffs of the Sringeri-maṭha, along with their names and period of reign, we see that it is only after Vidyāraṇya that the maṭha has stuck to the 'Bhārati' title (belonging to the Sringeri-maṭha) more strictly. This too is seen only until His Holiness Śrī Chandrashekhara Bharati (III) Mahaswami. The other pontiffs have, interestingly, been given titles of 'Tīrtha', 'Giri' and 'Araṇya' as well, which belong to the other three maṭhas, as per the above details from the *Maṭhāmnāya*. Also, when we look at the records of pontiffs of the Govardhan-maṭha, we find that most pontiffs have a title of 'Tīrtha' (belonging to the Dwarka-maṭha) and many others do not seem to have a title! The current head of the Govardhana-maṭha is His Holiness Śrī Nishcalananda Saraswati, who has a title that belongs to Sringeri-maṭha! The current head of the Dwarka-maṭha is His Holiness Śrī Sadananda Saraswati (earlier Ācārya was Swarupanand Saraswati) and that of Jyotirmaṭha is His Holiness Śrī Avimukteshvarananda Saraswati, both of whom have titles 'Sarasvati' belonging to Sringeri-maṭha. Beyond these, when we look at the titles of the Ācāryas of Kanchi-maṭha, we find the title 'Indra Sarasvati' in all their names.

All this leads us to believe that though the *Maṭhāmnāya* speaks of certain titles for certain maṭhas, in practice they were probably not followed so strictly by the maṭhas.

It may be also pointed out here that apart from the Sringeri-maṭha, the other Āmnāya-maṭhas have faced challenges in maintaining a continued lineage internally. In many cases, to ensure continuity, they have had to bring in saṁnyāsīs from outside the maṭha to head the maṭha. In these cases, we are bound to see mixing of the titles. A case in point is His Holiness Śrī Bharati Krishna Tirtha, who was initiated into saṁnyāsa by His Holiness Śrī Chandrashekhara Bharati Mahaswami of Sringeri and was brought in as the head of Dwarka-maṭha when there was no direct successor to the earlier Ācārya. Same is the case of His Holiness Śrī Swarupanand Saraswati who was heading both Dwarka-maṭha and Jyotirmaṭha. Interested readers can get a list of all the Jagadgurus who adorned the various Āmnāya-maṭhas in S.S. Saraswati (2015, pp. 516–55).

Most of the information on the functioning of the maṭhas seems to be from the *Maṭhāmnāya*. Now what is the *Maṭhāmnāya* all about?

Maṭhāmnāya

Maṭhāmnāya, also called *Maṭhāmnāya-setu* or *Mahānuśāsanam*, is a set of seventy-five verses attributed to Śaṅkara instructing the functioning of the four Āmnāya-maṭhas. This is probably the only extant text that focuses on the functions and other details of the 'maṭha' and the heads of the maṭha. It may be worth mentioning here that there are quite a few contentions on the authorship and date of this text. Some opine this to be the work of king Sudhanvā and belonging to a much later time than Śaṅkara.

The text starts with describing the four Āmnāya-maṭhas by giving details of their names, the titles of saṁnyāsīs associated, the territories governed by the maṭhas, the deities to be worshipped by the maṭha, the sacred river associated with the maṭha, as well as the Veda-śākhā and Mahāvākya (from the Upaniṣads) associated with the maṭha. The text then goes on to lay the qualities for the head of the maṭha. Interestingly, here it is said that a pontiff with the required qualities assuming the headship of the maṭha must be seen as Śaṅkara himself. It is hence probably that unlike other traditions, all the descendants of the four Āmnāya-maṭhas are referred to by the general term 'Śaṅkarācārya', though in reality, it belongs to Ādi Śaṅkara Bhagavatpāda alone. The text also prohibits the appointment of multiple disciples as successors.

The table below gives details of the four Āmnāya-maṭhas as per *Maṭhāmnāya*:

Āmnāya	Maṭha	Kṣetra	Veda	Ācārya	Tīrtha	Devatā	Śaktī
Paścima-āmnāya	Śāradā[3]	Dwarka	Sāma-veda	Hastāmalaka	Gomati	Siddheśvara	Bhadrakālī
Pūrva-āmnāya	Govardhana	Puri/ Puruṣottama	Ṛgveda	Padmapāda	Mahodadhi (Bay of Bengal)	Jagannātha	Vimalā
Uttara-āmnāya	Jyotirmaṭha[4]	Badari	Atharva-veda	Toṭaka	Alakananda	Nārāyaṇa	Pūrṇagirī
Dakṣiṇa-āmnāya	Sringeri	Rameshwaram	Yajur-veda	Sureśvara	Tunga-bhadra	Ādi-varāha	Kāmākṣī[5]

As regards the assignment of the Vedas to the four Āmnāya-maṭhas, one possibility is that these were the Veda śākhās to which the respective disciples of the Ācārya belonged. Swami Chinmayananda, in his book, validates the point for Sureśvara, stating that he belonged to *Śukla-yajurveda* and hence Ācārya asked him to write the vārtika for his bhāṣya on *Bṛhadāraṇyaka-upaniṣad*, which belongs to *Śukla-yajurveda*, and on the *Taittirīya-upaniṣad* from *Kṛṣṇa-yajurveda* to which Ācārya himself belonged to.

A Note on Kanchi-maṭha

There has been a great debate in the recent past on whether Kanchi-maṭha was established by Ācārya. Below are a few thoughts on this:

1. We have established earlier that Ācārya did stay in Kanchi for a long time. BA also states that he established a maṭha here for the propagation of Sanātana-dharma.[6]
2. While the above *Maṭhāmnāya* does not explicitly mention of a Kanchi-maṭha, it says that the devī of the Sringeri-maṭha is Kāmākśī.[7] It may also be noted that for the other three Āmnāya-maṭhas, the kṣetra, devata and devī, all belong to the same place (Dwarka–Siddheśvara–Bhadrakālī; Puruṣottama–Jagannātha–Vimalā; Badarikāśram–Nārāyaṇa–Pūrṇagirī). Only for the Dakṣiṇāmnāya-maṭha, kṣetra is Rāmeśvara, devatā is varāha and devī is Kāmākśī while maṭha is in Sringeri!
3. We find another *Maṭhāmnāya* that is said to form the thirteenth prakaraṇa of *BSV*. Herein, beyond the details

of the four Āmnāya-maṭhas discussed above, Kanchi is mentioned as a Mukhya-āmnāya-maṭha established by Ācārya in the seat of Parāśaktī, which is Kāmakoṣṭha (another name for Kanchi). This is also called the Śāradā-maṭha, with kṣetra, devata and devī as Satyavrata (another name for Kanchi), Ekāmranātha and Śrī Kāmākoṭī, respectively. Interestingly, this also mentions that the successors of this Pītha do have the titles of 'Indra-sarasvati' or 'Bharati'.

4. We find records of an unbroken lineage of saṁnyāsīs adorning this Pītha. One important source of this is the *Jagadguru-ratna-mālā-stava* (or *Guru-ratna-mālikā*) of Sadāśiva Brahmendra. It begins by invocation to Brahman and then has invocations to each guru of the guru-paramparā, starting from Dakṣiṇāmūrti until his guru Paramaśivendra-sarasvati, which matches exactly with the records of the Kanchi-maṭha until the fifty-seventh Jagadguru Paramaśivendra-sarasvati. Herein, Brahmendra says that Ācārya established the Śāradā-maṭha in Kanchi.[8] Sadāśiva Brahmendra was one of the greatest realised souls of the last century.
5. While the proposition that there are two Dakṣiṇāmnāya-maṭhas is unacceptable, it could very well be considered that while Sringeri was the Dakṣiṇāmnāya-maṭha, Kanchi was an important maṭha established by the Ācārya called variedly as Mukhya-āmnāya, Madhyama-āmnāya or Mūla-āmnāya.

Śāstradhārī and Astradhārī Saṁnyāsīs

The Daśanāmī order of saṁnyāsīs was primarily started by Śaṅkara for the protection and propagation of Sanātana-dharma. During the time of Śaṅkara, only intellectual debates and logical arguments were needed to convince people to follow the Dharma and keep away the harmful elements. However, in later times, we saw ruthless and brutal invaders attacking Bhārata. These could not be dealt with intellectual arguments alone, and therefore, there was a need for physical combat. While this was primarily done by the Kṣatriya class, the Daśanāmī saṁnyāsīs of the north also played a significant role in this.

The Daśanāmī saṁnyāsīs were primarily classified as Śāstradhārī (bearers of spiritual and religious knowledge) and Astradhārī (bearers of weapons). This was not a mutually exclusive classification and most Astradhārī saṁnyāsīs were also trained in śāstras, while the reverse was not always true. Śāstradhārī saṁnyāsīs are commonly called daṇḍī saṁnyāsīs as they carry a staff, while the astradhārī saṁnyāsīs are called Nāgā sadhus. Nāgā sadhus are naked, carry a tri-daṇḍa (three-pronged staff) and smear their naked body with ashes. This is differentiated with the daṇḍī saṁnyāsīs who carry an eka-daṇḍa (single staff) and only apply the tri-puṇḍra (three horizontal lines of bhasma) on various parts of their body.

Astradhārī saṁnyāsīs are typically recruited through fifty-two Marhis (literally meaning a recruiting centre) based on their fulfilling the eligibility criteria to become a Daśanāmī saṁnyāsī. These Marhis are associated with

Akhārās, which imparted education on martial arts as well as knowledge of scriptures. There are seven akhārās that belong to the Daśanāmī saṁnyāsīs. These are Āvāhan, Aṭal, Agni, (Mahā) Nirvāṇī, Nirañjanī, Jūnā and Ānand. Of these, all the Akhārās, except Agni, take one of the ten names of Daśanāmī order, while the Agni Akhārā takes the titles given to Brahmacārīs in the *Maṭhāmnāya*, i.e., Svarūpa, Prakāśa, Ānanda or Caitanya. The hierarchy within the Akhārā is (from bottom to top): Mahant → Śrī Mahant → Mahāmaṇḍaleśvara and then a Śaṅkarācārya as the nominal head at the apex. While every Akhārā has at least one Mahāmaṇḍaleśvara associated with it, it is not essential that every Mahāmaṇḍaleśvara needs to be associated with an Akhārā. In fact, less than a third of Mahāmaṇḍaleśvaras are associated with an Akhārā. Like the maṭhas, the Akhārā also have their tutelary deities such as Kapila muni for (Mahā) Nirvāṇī, Kārtikeya for Nirañjanī, etc.

Śāstradhārī or daṇḍī saṁnyāsīs are initiated by other daṇḍī-maṭhas that are typically associated with one of the Āmnāya-maṭhas. Every daṇḍī-maṭha has a head called Mahant. All the daṇḍī-maṭhas in a district constitute a Maṇḍala, which has a head called Mahāmaṇḍaleśvara. Many of the Mahants and Maṇḍaleśvara have set up their own maṭhas and colleges of learning.

Beyond the śāstradhārī and astradhārī saṁnyāsīs are the Paramahaṁsas who are initiated by the Mahāmaṇḍaleśvara of any of the Akhārās and have their own maṭhas.

The astradhārī saṁnyāsīs (of the Akhārās) were also called the 'fighting monks' who fought many battles, such as the one against the Mughals to protect the Kashi Viśvanāth temple and Jñāna vāpi. They also rendered support to Peshwa Nanasaheb and Rani of Jhansi in the 1857 War of Independence. Currently, while the astradhārī saṁnyāsīs are still trained in physical training, wrestling, etc., they no more wield weapons as they did in the past.

Most of the Akhārās today do not have any connection with the maṭhas, both Āmnāya and otherwise, except for the fact that all of them trace their origin to Śaṅkara.

Maṭhas Initiated by the Āmnāya-maṭhas

Sringeri Mātha mentions of the tenth Jagadguru Vidyātīrtha making eight of his disciples (Śrī Saccidānanda, Śrī Advaita Brahmānanda (Bharatī Tīrtha), Śrī Sāndrananda, Śrī Advaitānanda Śevadhi, Śrī Mahādeva Śiva, Śrī Advaita Sukhānanda, Śrī Śivayogi, and Śrī Pratyagjyoti) as heads of eight maṭhas established by him. *Śaṅkara-vijaya-cūrṇikā* mentions of seven maṭhas as subsidiary maṭhas of Sringeri-maṭha. These are Virūpākṣa-maṭha, Puṣpagiri-maṭha, Kumbakoṇa-maṭha, Kūḍaligi-maṭha, Saṅkeśvara-maṭha, Śrī Śaila-maṭha and Āmaṇi (Āvaṇi)-maṭha. *Tamil Encyclopedia* also validates these names as maṭhas initiated by Sringeri-maṭha, except Kūḍaligi, Saṅkeśvara and Śrī Śaila. Instead, it adds Śivagaṅgā and Kākarla. Some of these might have been among the eight maṭhas established by Vidyātīrtha. There is another maṭha in Tīrthamuttūr on the banks of the river Tunga, centred on the Yoga Nṛsiṁha Svāmi temple, which is attributed to Vidyāraṇya.

Other References

The *Maṭhāmnāya* section of *BSV* speaks of Āmnāya aṣṭakam, i.e., eight Āmnāya-maṭhas. Beyond the four Āmnāya-maṭha discussed above, Kanchi Kāmakoṭi maṭha is mentioned as the Mukhya-āmnāya and Kaṣhi Sumeru Maṭha as Ūrdhva-āmnāya. Then, there are two other Āmnāya-maṭhas that seem more mystical and experiential in nature rather than physical. These are the Paramātmā-maṭha in Ātmā-āmnāya and Śuddha-śāṣtrārthaja-maṭha in Niṣkala-āmnāya. Beyond these, there is also a mention of Karavīra-pīṭha at Kolhapur and Dattātreya Pīṭha at Mahur.

Maṭhas of Kerala

After the samādhi of the Ācārya, the then king (probably a Cera Perumāḷ) of Thrissur (identified by some scholars as Rājaśekhara, mentioned in the MSV, who is said to have built the temple of Vadakkunnathan) is said to have established four maṭhas near the Vadakkunnathan temple and requested the four primary disciples of Ācārya, who were present during the samādhi, to adorn these. This could very well have been inspired by the Āmnāya-maṭhas established by the Ācārya in the four corners of Bhārata. However, because Kerala (and Thrissur) have more of an elongated structure, the East–West–North–South directions changed into North–Between–Central–South. These were the Vaḍakke (northern)-maṭham with Toṭaka, Iḍayil (in between)-maṭham with Hastāmalaka, Naḍuvil (Central)-maṭham with Sureśvara, and Thekke (southern)-maṭham with Padmapāda. Because the disciples had other responsibilities, including taking care of the Āmnāya-maṭhas that Ācārya had established and given charge to them, they initiated other Nambūdiri Brāhmaṇas into saṁnyāsa and handed these maṭhas to them. Thus began the tradition of Advaita-vedānta in Kerala. The maṭham is called as 'Swamiyar-maṭham' and the head is called the Muppil-swamiyar. While all these maṭhams were established in Thrissur, they moved to various other places over time.

Maṭha	Āmnāya	Ācārya	Upāsanā Mūrti
Iḍayil-maṭham	Ṛgveda	Hastāmalaka	Śrī Rāma
Naḍuvil-maṭham	Yajurveda	Sureshwara	Pārthasārathi
Vaḍakke-maṭham	Sāmaveda	Toṭaka	Dakṣiṇāmūrti
Thekke-maṭham	Atharva Veda	Padmapāda	Narasimha

Naḍuvil-maṭham

As regards Naḍuvil-maṭham, it is believed that Sureśvara appointed Vilvamaṅgalam-swamiyar as the head of Naḍuvil-maṭham. Vilvamaṅgalam is the name of a Nambūdiri family. There are believed to be two such Nambūdiri families – one in Shukapuram and other in Panniyur. Vilvamaṅgalam-swamiyar of Naḍuvil-maṭham is said to have belonged to the Shukapuram family and was known as Divākara śarmā (or Divākara muni) in his householder-life. Vilvamaṅgalam-swamiyar is a very popular personality in the religious history of Kerala and is associated with most of the important shrines in the state. There are scholars who opine that there have been multiple individuals with the name Vilvamaṅgalam spanning centuries.

Vilvamaṅgalam-swamiyar is considered as the one responsible for making the Ananta-padmanābha manifest in Tiru-ananta-puri (Trivandrum), and hence his successors (i.e., the Naḍuvil-maṭham swamiyars) alone have the right to perform Puṣpāñjali (flower worship) to Lord Ananta-padmanābha. They also received royal patronage. Naḍuvil-maṭham continues to function today, both in Thrissur and Travancore.

Vaḍakke-maṭham

The lineage of the Vaḍakke-maṭham is said to have ceased around four–five centuries ago when the then swamiyar, due to some reason, decided not to accept any disciple. He gave away all the properties and wealth held by the maṭham to the establishment of a Vedic school in Thrissur, which came to be called the Brahmasvam-maṭham. The Brahmasvam-maṭham continues to function to this day, imparting Vedic education to Nambūdiri Brāhmaṇas. The swamiyar is then said to have travelled to Kasargode enroute his journey to Kashi and stayed there for a cāturmāsya vrata. He was then requested by the local community to stay there permanently and bless them. Overcome by their devotion, he decided to stay back and established, what is today called, the Edaneer-maṭham. Because of its proximity to Karnataka, the heads of the Edaneer-maṭham are mostly Śivalli Brāhmaṇas hailing from Tulunad. Thus, the original Vaḍakke-maṭham is no more extant and exists today in the form of Edaneer-maṭham.

Iḍayil-maṭham

With the Travancore dynasty having the presence of a swamiyar from the Śaṅkara paramparā in their kingdom, the Zamorin of Calicut also felt the need to have the same in his kingdom. He hence invited the Iḍayil-maṭham-swamiyar to shift base from Thrissur to Trikkaikat. However, due to the later Islamic invasions, Iḍayil-maṭham-swamiyar had to evacuate Trikkaikat and take refuge in Travancore, where he was offered protection, royal patronage, space at Munchira in Kanyakumari, and given the responsibility to be the Puṣpāñjali-swamiyar for Padmanābha jointly with the Naḍuvil-maṭham-swamiyars. This marked the establishment of the Munchira-maṭham, which is but a branch of the Iḍayil-maṭham. Trikkaikat-maṭham also continues to function as an independent branch of Iḍayil-maṭham.

Thekke-maṭham

Thekke-maṭham continues to function in Thrissur as a swamiyar-maṭham. The Muppil-swamiyar of the Thekke-maṭham is the Puṣpāñjali-swamiyar of the Vadakkunnathan temple.

Maṭhas of Karnataka

Kudali Sringeri Mahāsaṁsthāna

There have been a lot of controversies between the Kudali-maṭha and Sringeri-maṭha on the rightful ownership of the Dakṣiṇāmnāya-maṭha established by Ādi Śaṅkara. Interestingly, the *Maṭhāmnāya* mentions the tīrtha for

Dakṣiṇāmnāya-maṭha as Tunga-bhadra, which is the place where the Kudali-maṭha is situated, while the Sringeri-maṭha is situated on the banks of the river Tunga! The term Kudali itself indicates 'confluence', i.e., the confluence of rivers Tunga and Bhadra. The maṭha has a list of seventy-two pīṭhādhipatis in their guru-paramparā, around the same as what we see at the Kanchi-maṭha and Dwarka-maṭha. The vigraha of Goddess Śāradā that we find in the Kudali-maṭha is in a standing posture holding the akṣamālā (rosary beads), a white lotus, abhaya mudrā, and a book in her four hands, while the Goddess in Sringeri is seated in padmāsana holding akṣamālā, a pot of nectar, cin-mudrā, and a book in her four hands.

Shakatapuram Shri Vidyapeetam

This maṭha is called 'Śrī Jagadguru Badari Śaṅkarācārya Samsthanam, Shakatapuram Shri Vidyapeetam'. As is evident from the name, the maṭha is a branch of the Uttarāmnāya-Śaṅkara-maṭha. Records suggest that during foreign invasions in the north around the 14th century, the then pontiff of Uttarāmnāya-jyotirmaṭha evacuated the maṭha and came down south in search of a place where he could continue his dharmic activities undisturbed. He selected Shakatapuram on the banks of the river Tunga in Karnataka as the right place for this and established his paramparā there.

Śrī Ramachandrapura-maṭha

This maṭha is said to have been established by the Ācārya in a place called Aśoke near Gokarna during his stay there.

This maṭha is also called Raghūttama-maṭha where Sureśvara appointed a disciple Vidyānanda as the first Ācārya.

Other Maṭhas

Some other maṭhas that are mentioned in this region are – Harihara-maṭha and Bhandigeḍi-maṭha in Koppa, Yogānandeśvara Maṭha in Holenarasīpura, Kodaṇḍāśrama-maṭha in Hebbur, Balekuduru-maṭha in Udupi, Honnavalli-maṭha in Sirasi, Chitrāpura-maṭha in Shirali and Cintāmaṇi-maṭha in Hospet.

Maṭhas of Goa

Kelosi in Goa is mentioned to have the Kaivalya-maṭha. We also see the Gauḍapādācārya-maṭha in Kavale. Though not a Śaṅkara-maṭha, it belongs to another lineage of Śaṅkara's parama-guru Gauḍapādācārya; hence the mention.

Ramakrishna Mission

In the life of Ramakrishna Paramahamsa, we find the arrival of a saṁnyāsī called Totapuri, who is said to have initiated Ramakrishna into the final state of nirvikalpa-samādhi. This saṁnyāsī belonged to the Daśanāmi-sampradāya with the title 'Puri'. Since 'Puri' is a title allocated to the Sringeri-maṭha as per the *Maṭhāmnāya*, the saṁnyāsīs of the Ramakrishna order consider themselves as descendents of the Sringeri-maṭha tradition of Śaṅkara. Sarkar (2022) mentions that Totapuri was the Mahant of the Mahā-nirvāṇī-akhārā for nearly six years.

Divine Life Society: Chinmaya Mission – Arsha Vidya Gurukula

Swami Sivananda (Saraswati), founder of the Divine Life Society, took initiation from Swami Vishvananda Saraswati who belonged to the Sringeri-maṭha tradition. Swami Chinmayananda (Saraswati), the founder of the Chinmaya Mission, was a disciple of Swami Sivananda and was initiated into saṁnyāsa by him. Swami Dayananda Saraswati, who later founded the Arsha Vidya gurukula, was the disciple of Swami Chinmayananda. Brahmacārīs of the four Āmnāya-maṭhas were also given specific titles, of which Chaitanya was the title for Sringeri-maṭha. This is followed even today by the Chinmaya Mission for all its brahmacārīs.

Datta Sampradāya

Nṛsiṁha Sarasvatī, who is considered to be an incarnation of Dattātreya, and is revered greatly in the Datta sampradaya, belonged to the Daśanāmī order and comes in the Sringeri lineage as mentioned in the guru-caritra. The line of Jagadgurus is common until Vidyāraṇya, after which we have the lineage given as Vidyāraṇya → Śrīpādamuni → Vidyātīrtha → Maliānanda → Devatīrtha → Sarasvatī tirtha (vṛnda) → Yādavendra Sarasvatī → Kṛṣṇa Sarasvatī → Nṛsiṁha Sarasvatī.

Ramana Maharshi

Ramana Maharshi was a realised soul, a brahma-jñānī of the highest order that we witnessed in the last century.

Though not belonging to any tradition or paramparā, Maharshi mentions, in his introduction to the Tamizh translation of Ācārya's *Dakṣiṇāmūrti-stotram*, that it is Śaṅkara himself in the form of Ramana who is commencing to write this![9]

Literary Traditions

Beyond the monastic traditions, we have a much bigger literary tradition of Śaṅkara that followed (and continues to follow) the path laid by the Ācārya.

Brahma-sūtra-bhāṣya (Śārīraka-bhāṣya)

Some of the significant names in that tradition who wrote vyākhyās on Ācārya's *Brahma-sūtra-bhāṣya* are Padmapāda, who wrote the commentary on the *adhyāsa-bhāṣya* and first four sūtras called *Pañcapādikā*; Vācaspati Miśra, who wrote *Bhāmati*, which is the first full-fledged commentary on Ācārya's bhāṣya; Rāmānanda who wrote *Bhāṣya-ratna-prabhā*; and Ānandajñāna, who wrote *Nyāya-nirṇaya*. Uttamajña wrote the *Vaktavya-kāsikā* on the *Pañcapādikā*, while Pūrṇānanda Sarasvatī wrote the *Pūrṇānandīya* on the *Bhāṣya-ratna-prabhā*. Commentaries on *Bhāmati* include *Vedānta-kalpataru* by Amalānanda and *Bhāmati-vyākhyā* by Akhaṇḍānanda. Appayya Dīkṣita wrote *Parimaḷa*, which is a commentary on the *Vedānta-kalpataru*.

Historian, archaeologist and epigraphist Dr R. Nagaswamy records the finding of a Cola inscription, dating to the reign of Vīra Rājendra Cola of 11th century CE, in the Kailasanātha temple in Colamahādevī village of Tamil Nadu. The inscription in Tamizh language and script, with a few Sanskrit words written in grantha characters, records the gift of land to scholars of the villages expounding a commentary on the *Brahma-sūtra-śāṅkara-bhāṣya* (mentioned as *Bhagavatpādīyam* in the inscription) called *Pradīpaka* written by one Cidānanda-bhaṭṭāra. This speaks of the popularity the works of the Ācārya enjoyed in the Cola deśa during the 10th–11th century CE.

Upaniṣad bhāṣya

Sureśvara wrote the vārtika for the *Taittirīya-upaniṣad* and *Bṛhadāraṇyaka-upaniṣad-bhāṣyas*, earning the title of 'vārtika-kāra'. We also have a commentary called *Vanamāla* by Acyuta Kṛṣṇānanda tīrtha on the *Taittirīya-upaniṣad-bhāṣya* of the Ācārya. Beyond these, we have the tīkā by Ānandagiri for all the ten Upaniṣad bhāṣyas (except *Nṛsiṁha-tāpani-upaniṣad*) of the Ācārya.

Bhagavad Gītā-bhāṣya

On the *Bhagavad Gītā-bhāṣya* of the Ācārya, we only have the tīkā by Ānandagiri.

Other works

Among many other works based on the Advaita-siddhānta of Śaṅkara, we have *Advaita-siddhi* by Madhusūdana Sarasvatī and *Śāstra-siddhānta-leśa-saṅgraha* of Appayya Dīkṣita.

Living Traditions

Beyond the living traditions of Ācārya related to temple worship and monastic orders, as seen earlier, there are many living traditions attributed to the Ācārya that are followed till day in the religious lives of the people of Sanātana-dharma.

One example of this is the pañcāyatana pūjā, which is the worship of five deities on a single pedestal. These are Gaṇeśa (in the form of red stone from the river Śoṇabhadra or Son), Śiva (in the form of bāṇa-liṅga from the river Narmada), Śaktī (in form of a stone from the river Suvarnamukhī), Viṣṇu (in the form of sālagrāma from the river Gandaki), and Sūrya (in the form of sphaṭika or crystal). This finds mention in PSV as well.[10] Though as theistic traditions, in addition to the above five, Śaṅkara also propagated the Kaumāra tradition (worship of Kumara or Subrahmaṇya) – Subrahmaṇya was not included in the pañcāyatana pūjā as he was worshipped in the form of fire in every Brāhmaṇa household.[11] With the dwindling away of the performance of fire rituals in later days, many families have included Subrahmaṇya into the pūjā in the form of a spear (vēl) or a serpent form (nāga-biṁba). The deities are arranged on the pedestal in such a way that the iṣṭa-devatā of the individual is placed in the centre and other deities surround it. The intent of this pūjā is to ensure that while the individual continues to surrender to his/her iṣṭa-devatā, he/she also worships all the other deities with respect and devotion, thus eschewing any animosity.

Ācārya is also attributed with the introduction of the mantra 'Mamopātta-samasta-durita-kṣaya-dvārā-śrī-parameśvara-prītyartham' that is chanted before any saṅkalpa, to bring in a sense of surrender and devotion in people, as opposed to the pride of performing the karma!

ADHYĀYA 18

The Inspiration That Is Śaṅkara

असद्धूमकेतो त्रयीधर्मकेतो नमः शङ्कराचार्य सद्धर्मसेतो |
तमः पद्मबन्धो सदाचारबन्धो नमः शङ्कराचार्य कारुण्यसिन्धो ||

Prostrations to Śaṅkarācārya who is like a comet (destroyer) to the vice, who is the flag bearer of the Vedic dharma, who is the bridge leading us to the right dharma, who is the like sun to the darkness (of ignorance), who is a friend of the virtuous, who is an ocean of compassion.

—*Bhagavatpāda-abhyudaya* 9.111

At a time when the survival of Sanātana-dharma was threatened by various other faiths and beliefs, Ācārya walked through the length and breadth of Bhārata, and through his sharp intellect, intense devotion to the śāstras and a compassionate heart, transformed the land, making it suitable for the flourishing of Sanātana-dharma, the benefits of which we and our ancestors have been reaping. The story, however, has not ended. Even today, there continue to be attacks on Sanātana-dharma and threats to destroy it. While the Ācārya is no more in flesh and blood with us, He continues to live in spirit in all the faithful hearts, as an eternal inspiration! May He continue to inspire our intellects and direct them such that we are able to stand up to protect and sustain our Sanātana-dharma.

भव शङ्कर देशिक मे शरणम्

O Preceptor Śaṅkara, be my refuge!

APPENDIX 1

Śaṅkara's Digvijaya Yātrā Map with References

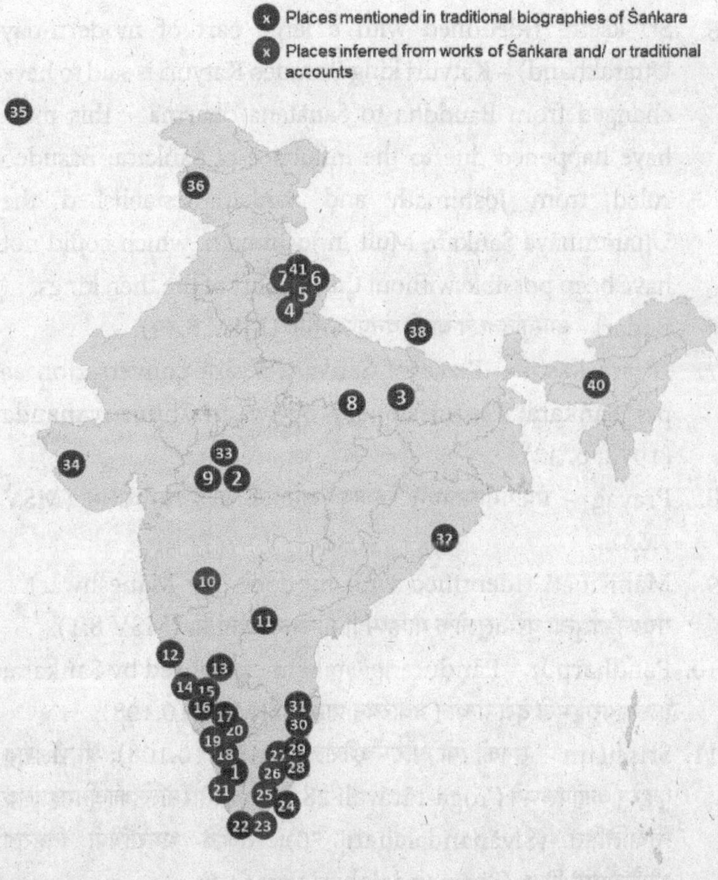

1. Kalady – अग्रहारः काल्ट्यभिख्योस्ति (MSV 2.3).
2. Omkareshwar (banks of the river Narmada) - प्रपेदे नर्मदातटम् (BA 3.74); the caves on the Māndhātā island depict the episode of Śaṅkara meeting Govinda Bhagavatpāda and controlling the fury of Narmada.
3. Kashi - प्राप तापसवरः स हि काशीं (MSV 5.165).
4. Rishikesh – reconsecrating of Hṛṣīkeśa Nārāyaṇa on Basant-pañcamī is attributed to Śaṅkara; http://shribharatmandir.org/preface.
5. Śri kṣetra (identified with a large part of modern-day Uttarakhand) – Katyuri king Basudeo Katyuri is said to have changed from Bauddha to Sanātana-dharma – this must have happened due to the influence of Śaṅkara; Basudeo ruled from Joshimath and Śaṅkara established the Uttarāmnāya Śaṅkara Mutt in Joshimath, which could not have been possible without the support of the then kings.
6. Badari - आसादिता च बदरी वनपुण्यभूमिः (MSV 6.59).
7. Uttara-kashi – Place of Śaṅkara-Vyāsa conversation as per 'Śaṅkara: The missionary' by Swami Chinmayananda (1978, p. 32).
8. Prayag – प्रयागमागत्प्रथमं जिगीषुः कुमारिलं साधितकर्मजालम् (MSV 7.62).
9. Māhiśmatī (identified with modern-day Maheshwar) – गच्छन् खसृत्या पुरमालुलोके माहिष्मतीं मण्डनमण्डितां सः (MSV 8.1).
10. Pandharpur – Pāṇḍuraṅgāṣṭakam composed by Śaṅkara; तत्र महाराष्ट्रमुखे देशे ग्रन्थान् प्रचारयन् प्राज्ञतमः (MSV 10.108).
11. Srisailam – सनकोपमो आगमच्छ्रीशैलम् (MSV 10.108); श्री शैलशृङ्ग कुहरेषु कदोपलप्स्ये (Yoga-tārāvali 28); सेवे श्रीगिरिमल्लिकार्जुनमहालिङ्गं शिवालिङ्गितं (Śivānandalahari 50); राजीवे भ्रमराधिपो विहरतां श्रीशैलवासी विभुः (Śivānandalahari verse 51).

12. Gokarna – आगात्गोकर्णमभ्यर्णचलार्णवौघम् (MSV 12.1).
13. Harihar – हरिशङ्कराख्यम् (MSV 12.7).
14. Mookambika – मूकाम्बिकायाः सदनं प्रतस्थे (MSV 12.20).
15. Śribali – अग्रहारकं श्रीबलिसंज्ञं (MSV 12.39).
16. Sringeri – शृङ्गगिरिं प्रतस्थे (MSV 12.63).
17. Kukke Subrahmanya – सुब्रह्मण्यप्रियावासं सुब्रह्मण्यस्थलं ययौ | नद्यां कुमारधारायां तत्र स्नात्वा गुरूत्तमः (BA 8.114); स्नात्वा कुमारधारायां नद्यां शिष्यसमन्वितः भक्त्या संपूजयामास षण्मुखं शेषरूपिणम् (PSV Ch. 11).
18. Vadakkunnathan temple – the temple has a samadhi for Śaṅkara based on the more popular belief in Kerala that Śaṅkara attained samadhi within this temple.
19. Guruvayur – The Tantris have ascertained that the Tāntric rituals of the temple were codified and handed over to their ancestors by Śaṅkara.
20. Kadampuzha – popular belief is that Śaṅkara discovered the sanctity of this temple; https://www.kadampuzhadevaswom.com/.
21. Chottanikkara temple – popular belief is that Śaṅkara brought the sanctity of the Goddess in this place; https://chottanikkarabhagavathy.org/history.php.
22. Tiruvanantapuram – प्रवर्तयन् वेदमार्गे ततो अनन्तपुरं ययौ (BA 8.99).
23. Tiruchendur–Subrahmaṇya–bhujaṅgam (SB) was composed by Śaṅkara at this temple – महाम्भोधितीरे महापापचोरे मुनीन्द्रानुकूले सुगन्धाख्यशैले (SB 7).
24. Rameshwaram – अभिपूज्य स तत्र रामनाथं (MSV 15.4); चतुर्थो दक्षिणाम्नाय शृङ्गेरि तु मठो भवेत्...रामेश्वराह्वयं क्षेत्रं (Mathanushasanam, verses 28–29).
25. Madurai – Mīnākṣī-pañcaratnam composed by Śaṅkara.
26. Srirangam – Rañganathāṣṭakam composed by Śaṅkara.

27. Jambukeshwaram – consecration of śri-cakra tāṭaṅka for Devi Akhilāṇḍeśvarī and subsequent tradition of replacing them by Śaṅkarācāryas of Kanchi Mutt.
28. Tiruvidaimarudur – मध्यार्जुनं गतः | स्नात्वा कवेरकन्यायां महालिङ्गं स्तुवन् गुरुः | (BA 8.84-85); मध्यार्जुनेशः लिङ्गाग्रात् सावयवरूपेण निष्क्रम्य मेघवद्गम्भीरगिरा दक्षिणं हस्तमुद्यम्य सत्यमद्वैतं इति त्रिरुक्त्वा लिङ्गाग्रेणान्तर्दधे पश्यतां नराणां महदद्भुतमासीत् (PSV Ch. 4).
29. Chidambaram – शिवलिङ्गं प्रतिष्ठाप्य चिदम्बरसभातले (Markendeya Samhita referred to in *Adi Śaṅkara: His life and times* by His Holiness Śrī Chandrashekharendra Saraswati, p. 48).
30. Kanchipuram – ततो जगाम काञ्चीं नगरीं (MSV 15.4); श्रीचक्रं स्थापयामास कामाक्ष्याः पुरो गुरुः मठं च स्थापयामास तत्र विद्याभिवर्धये (BA 8.79); तस्मिन् स्थले मासमात्रं स्थित्वा शङ्कुप्रतिष्ठापूर्वकं शिवकाञ्चीति पट्टणं निर्माय ....परमगुरुः सुखमास (PSV Ch.63); https://www.kamakoti.org/kamakoti/details/Shankaracharya-Kanchipuram%20Home.html
31. Tirupati – स वेङ्कटाचलेशं प्रणिपात्य (MSV 15.6).
32. Puri – जगन्नाथः स्वामी नयनपथगामी भवतु मे (colophon in Jagannatha-ashtakam); पूर्वाम्नायो द्वितीयस्स्यात् गोवर्धनमठ स्मृतः ... पुरुषोत्तमं तु क्षेत्रं स्यात् जगन्नथोस्य देवता (Mathanushasanam, pp. 10–11); '*Sri Jagannath and Adi guru Shankaracharya*' – article in *Odisha Review*, June 2017, pp. 35–38.
33. Ujjain – उज्जयिनीं पुरीमयासीत् (MSV 15.76).
34. Dwarka – द्वारवतीं पुरीं विवेश (MSV 15.73); प्रथमः पश्चिमाम्नाय शारदामठ उच्यते ...द्वरकाख्यं हि क्षेत्रं स्यात् (Maṭhānuśāsanam, pp. 1–2).
35. Bāhlika (identified with Balkh) – प्रतिपाद्य तु बाह्लिकान् (MSV 15.142).
36. Kashmir – काश्मीरदेशाय जगाम हृष्टः श्रीशङ्करः (MSV 16.58).

37. Darada, Bharata, Śūrasena, Kuru, Pāñcāla - दरदान् भरतांश्च शूरसेनान् कुरुपाञ्चालमुखान् बहूनजैषीत् (MSV 15.156).
38. Paśupatināth (Nepal) – नीलकण्ठे वरेश्वरम् (Mārkaṇḍeya-saṁhitā referred to in *Adi Śaṅkara: His life and times* by His Holiness Śrī Chandrashekharendra Saraswati, p. 48); continued the practice/tradition of Bhaṭṭa (chief priest) of Pashupatinath temple being selected and sent from Karnataka after approval by Sringeri Mutt.
39. Videha, Kosala, Añga, Vañga, Gauḍa – विदेह-कौशलाद्यैः...अङ्ग-वङ्गेश्वयमास्तीर्य यशो जगाम गौडान् (MSV 16.161).
40. Kāmarūpa – तदनन्तरमेष कामरूपानधिगत्य (MSV 15.158).
41. Kedar – योगिबृन्दाधिपः प्राप केदारम् (MSV 16.100).

APPENDIX 2

Date of Śaṅkara: A Brief Note

The date of the Śaṅkara has been a topic of heated debate among scholars and others, with several estimates ranging from 5th century BCE (507 BCE) to 8th century CE (788 CE), i.e., thirteen hundred years apart! It seems to be a topic with no resolution, with different factions and scholars continuing to ascertain the estimates they believe in, references to which are mentioned in the bibliography for interested individuals. The author does not intend to get into this analysis in the scope of this book. As Swami Ramanacharana tirtha says, Ācārya himself has declared that he has neither birth nor death, neither mother nor father.[1] Then why bother of his year of birth? Knowing that is not going to change our devotion to him in any way, isn't it? However, for the benefit of the readers, the author intends to provide some pointers on this topic.

Ācārya, like the sages of yore, has not bothered to mention about his year of birth anywhere. He wanted his works on the Upaniṣadic teachings to be read, understood, assimilated and remembered. Not his date of birth. There are no literary mentions of his date by his contemporaries or his immediate successors. There is no inscriptional or epigraphical evidence as well in this regard. The 'so-called' available evidence, mostly literary, on the year of Ācārya belongs to much later periods. Hence, their authenticity needs to be looked at more deeply. Even the Śaṅkara-maṭhas have no unanimity on this topic, with Joshimath, Puri, Dwarka and Kanchi-maṭhas suggesting 5th century BCE while the Sringeri-maṭha suggesting 8th century CE. The point that most scholars agree upon is the chronology of Buddha–Kālidāsa–Kumārila Bhaṭṭa–Śaṅkara, with the last two being contemporaries. However, just like we are struggling to fix the year of the Ācārya, the years of Buddha and Kālidāsa are also shrouded in ambiguity and confusion. Even in their cases, there are popular versions, and lesser-known versions.

Despite these confusions, the author found the compilation of lectures of the Mahaswami of Kanchi (under the title *Deivathin Kural* in Tamizh and *Thus Spake the Divine* in English) to be extremely comprehensive and detailed in this regard (especially pages 680–749 of the 5th volume of *Thus Spake the Divine*). There is also a good compilation of the various views presented in S.S. Saraswati (2015, pp. 451–61). Interested readers could refer these.

APPENDIX 3

List of Śaṅkara's Works

Commentaries (Bhāṣya)

Upaniṣads

Īśa-upaniṣad

Kena-upaniṣad

Kaṭha-upaniṣad

Praśna-upaniṣad

Muṇḍaka-upaniṣad

Māṇḍūkya-upaniṣad

Taittirīya-upaniṣad

Aitareya-upaniṣad

Chāndogya-upaniṣad

Bṛhadāraṇyaka-upaniṣad

Nṛsiṁha-pūrva & uttara-tāpani-upaniṣad

Brahma-sūtras of Bādarāyaṇa (Śārīraka-bhāṣya)

Bhagavad Gītā

Others

Hastāmalakīya

Lalitā triśatī

Sanat-sujātīya

Viṣṇu-sahasranāma

Vedānta (smaller works from A–Z)

Advaita-pañcaratnam

Advaitānubhūtiḥ

Anātma-śrī-vigarhaṇam

Brahma-jñānāvalī-mālā

Brahmānucintanam

Daśaślokī

Dhanyāṣṭakam

Eka-ślokī

Jīvan-muktānanda-laharī

Laghu-vākya-vṛttiḥ

Manīṣā-pañcakam

Māyā-pañcakam

Nirvāṇa-mañjarī

Nirvāṇa-ṣaṭkam

Pañcīkaraṇam

Prabodha-sudhākaraḥ

Praśnottara-ratna-mālikā

Prauḍhānubhūtiḥ

Sadācārānusandhānam

Śata-ślokī

Svarūpānusandhāna-aṣṭakam

Vedānta (smaller works from A–Z) contd.

Svātma-nirūpaṇam

Svātmaprakāśikā

Tattva-bodha

Tattvopadeśaḥ

Upadeśa-pañcakam

Vākya-vṛttiḥ

Yati-pañcakam

Vedānta (bigger works)

Aparokṣānubhūtiḥ

Ātma-bodha

Sarva-vedānta- siddhānta-sāra-saṅgraha

Upadeśa-sāhasrī

Viveka-cūḍāmaṇiḥ

Yoga

Yoga tārāvali

Tantra

Prapañca-sāra-tantra

Stotra literature (A–Z)

Acyuta-aṣṭakam

Annapūrṇā-stutiḥ

Ardhanārīśvara-stotram

Ānanda-laharī

Bhavānī-bhujaṅgam

Bhagavan-mānasa-pūjā-stotram

Bhramarāmbāṣṭakam

Dakṣiṇāmūrti-stotram

Dakṣiṇāmūrti-varṇamālā-stotram

Daśaśloki-stutiḥ

Devī-bhujaṅga-stotram

Devī-catuṣaṣṭyupacāra-pūjā-stotram

Devyāparādha- kṣamāpaṇa-stotram

Dvādaśa-liṅga-stotram

Gaṇeśa bhujaṅgam

Ganga-aṣṭakam

Gaurī-daśakam

Govinda-aṣṭakam

Guru-aṣṭakam

Hanumat-pañcaratnam

Hari-stutiḥ

Jagannātha-aṣṭakam

Kālabhairava-aṣṭakam

Kalyāṇa-vṛṣṭi-stavaḥ

Kanaka-dhāra-stotram

Kashi-pañcakam

Kṛṣṇa-aṣṭakam

Stotra literature (A–Z) contd.

Lakṣmī-Nṛsiṁha-karuṇārasa-stotram

Lakṣmī-Nṛsiṁha-pañcaratnam

Maṇikarṇikā-aṣṭakam

Mantra-mātṛkā-puṣpa-mālā-stavaḥ

Mātṛ-pañcakam

Mīnākṣī-pañcaratnam

Mīnākṣī-stotram

Moha-mudgaraḥ (Bhaja Govindam)

Narmada-aṣṭakam

Navaratnamālikā

Nirguṇa- mānasa-pūjā

Pāṇḍuraṅga-aṣṭakam

Prātaḥ-smaraṇa-stotram

Saundarya-laharī

Śāradā-bhujaṅga-prayātāṣṭakam

Ṣaṭpadī-stotram

Śiva bhujaṅgam

Śiva-keśādi-pādānta-varṇana-stotram

Śiva-nāmāvalyaṣṭakam

Śivānandalaharī

Śiva-pādādi-keśānta-varṇana-stotram

Śiva-pañcakṣara-nakṣatra-mālā-stotram

Śiva-pañcakṣara-stotram

Śivāparādha-kṣamāpaṇa-stotram

Śrī Dakṣiṇāmūrti-aṣṭakam

Śrī Gaṇeśa pañcaratnam

Śrī-Lalitā-pañcaratnam

Śrī Mṛtyuñjaya-mānasika-pūjā-stotram

Śrī-Rāma-bhujaṅga-prayāta-stotram

Subrahmaṇya bhujaṅgam

Suvarṇa-mālā-stutiḥ

Tripurasundarī-aṣṭakam

Tripurasundarī-mānasa-pūjā-stotram

Tripurasundarī-veda-pāda-stotram

Umā-maheśvara-stotram

Viṣṇu-bhujaṅga-prayāta-stotram

Viṣṇu- pādādi-keśānta-stotram

Veda-sāra-Śiva-stotram

Yamunā-aṣṭakam

APPENDIX 4

List of Works on Śaṅkara

(Not exhaustive)

1. *Ācārya-vijaya* by Paramesvara Kavikaṇṭhīrava
2. *Bhagavatpādābhyudayam of Lakṣmaṇa Sūrī*
3. *Bhagavatpāda-saptati* by Jagannātha Kavi
4. *Bṛhat-*śaṅkara-*vijaya of Citsukhācārya* (not extant)
5. *Guru-vamśa-kāvyam* by Kashi Lakṣmaṇa Śāstrī
6. *Guru (or Jagadguru)-ratna-mālikā (or mālā-stava)* by Sadāśiva Brahmendra
7. *Keralīya-śaṅkara-vijaya (or* Śaṅkarācārya *Caritam or* Ācārya *Caritam)* of Govindanātha
8. *Madhavīya (or Saṁkṣepa)*-śaṅkara-vijaya of Vidyāraṇya along with *Advaita-rājya-lakṣmī ṭīkā* and *Ḍiṇḍimā vyākhyā* of Dhanapati Sūrī
9. *Mārkaṇḍeya-saṁhitā*, chapter 3 (part of *Brahmāṇḍa-purāṇa)*
10. *Patañjali-caritam* by Rāmabhadra Dīkṣita
11. *Prācīna-śaṅkara-vijaya* of Ānandagiri
12. *Puṅya-śloka-mañjari* by Sarvajña Sadāśivendra Sarasvati
13. *Śaṅkarābhyudaya of Rāja Cuḍāmaṇi Dīkṣita*
14. *Śaṅkarābhyudaya-kāvya of Nīlakaṇṭha*
15. *Śaṅkarābhyudaya-mahākāvya of Tirumala Dīkṣita*

16. *Śaṅkarācārya-mahimā* by Bālagopāla yati
17. *Śaṅkara-jīvanākhyānam* by Smt. Kshama Raghavendra Rao
18. *Śaṅkara-kathā-sudhā-nidhi* by Rāma Śarmā
19. *Śaṅkara-mandāra-saurabha of Nīlakaṇṭha*
20. *Śaṅkara-(dig)vijaya-sāra* by Sadānanda or Sadānandavyāsa
21. *Śaṅkara-(dig)vijaya-sāra* by Śrīnivāsa Kedilāya
22. *Śaṅkara-vijaya of Vyāsācala (or Vyāsācalīya)*
23. *Śaṅkara-vijaya (or Guru Vijaya or* Ācārya *Vijaya) of Anantānandagiri*
24. *Śaṅkaṛa-vijaya (or* Śaṅkarācārya *Campu) of Vallīsahāya*
25. *Śaṅkara-vijaya*-cūrṇikā by Gurunātha
26. *Śaṅkara vijaya-saṅgraha* by Puruṣottama Bhāratī
27. *Śaṅkara-vijaya*-vilāsa *of Cidvilāsa*
28. *Śaṅkarendra-vilāsa of Vākpati Bhaṭṭa*
29. *Śiva-rahasya*, 16th chapter of the 9th aṁśa *(Itihāsa)*

APPENDIX 5

Diacritics Chart

Sanskrit is typically written in the *Devanāgarī* script. To write Sanskrit using the Latin alphabet, we can use one of the many transliteration schemes available; the most popular is the International Alphabet of Sanskrit Transliteration (IAST), which is what is used in this book.

Letters of the Sanskrit Alphabet

अ	आ	इ	ई	उ	ऊ	ऋ	ॠ	ऌ	ए	ऐ	ओ	औ	अं	अः
a	ā	i	ī	u	ū	ṛ	ṝ	ḷ	e	ai	o	au	aṁ	aḥ

क्	ख्	ग्	घ्	ङ्
k	kh	g	gh	ṅ
च्	छ्	ज्	झ्	ञ्
c	ch	j	jh	ñ
ट्	ठ्	ड्	ढ्	ण्
ṭ	ṭh	ḍ	ḍh	ṇ
त्	थ्	द्	ध्	न्
t	th	d	dh	n
प्	फ्	ब्	भ्	म्
p	ph	b	bh	m

य्	र्	ल्	व्	श्	ष्	स्	ह्
y	r	l	v	ś	ṣ	s	h

Pronunciation of the Vowels

a as in apart	*ā* as in are
i as in in	*ī* as in free
u as in good	*ū* as in mood
ṛ as in rhythm	*ṝ* is rri (rolled)
e as in bay	*ai* as in fly
o as in old	*au* as in owl
aṁ as in hum	*aḥ* is a-huh

Pronunciation of the Consonants

k as in kid	*g* as in get	*ṅ* as in song
c as in chat	*j* as in joy	*ñ* as in inch
ṭ as in toy	*ḍ* as in day	*ṇ* as in end
t as in thin	*d* as in this	*n* as in now
p as in pub	*b* as in bag	*m* as in map

Pronunciation of the Half-vowels

y as in yam	*r* as in rig
l as in leg	*v* as in van
ś as in shy	*s* as in sit
h as in how	

The sound for the vowel *ḷ* does not exist in English. *kh*, *gh*, *ch*, *jh*, *ṭh*, *ḍh*, *th*, *dh*, *ph*, *bh* are aspirated versions of *k*, *g*, *c*, *j*, *ṭ*, *ḍ*, *t*, *d*, *p*, *b*. The half-vowel *ṣ* does not exist in English; it is approximately like an aspirated version of *ś*.

APPENDIX 6

Glossary

abhaya-mudra	hand gesture suggesting protection from fear
ācārya	one who teaches, practices what he/she teaches and makes others practice the teaching; teacher of high stature
Advaita	monism on non-dualism
āgama	texts, other than the Vedic corpus, that deal with temples, rituals and worship of deities as well as spiritual practices for self-realisation
Āzhvār	term used for the twelve Vaiṣṇavite saints of Draviḍa-deśa who spread Viṣṇu-bhaktī, especially in the southern part of the country
āmnāya	refers to knowledge received through a tradition, especially the Vedas
Bhārata	the term used to refer to the larger Indian subcontinent that comprised ancient India
bhāṣya	commentary on a text that explains every line and word of the original text

bhikku	Buddhist ascetic; variation of the Sanskrit word 'bhikṣu', i.e., one who lives on bhikṣā
bhikṣā	providing food, primarily to saṁnyāsīs (who, being renunciates are not allowed to earn or hoard money) and brahmacārīs (who, being students, are focused on education and have not yet started earning money)
brahmacārī	a student undergoing education; one who adheres to physical continence and is constantly engaged in meditation on Brahman
brāhmaṇa	Brahmin; one of the four classifications/sections of Vedic society that focused on studying the Vedas, teaching the Vedas, performance of Vedic rituals and guiding others in performance of Vedic rituals
Brahman	the Supreme Being as referred to in the Upaniṣads
Brahmasūtra	aphorisms on Brahman
cakra	discus – one of the weapons of Lord Viṣṇu
caṇḍāla	one of the communities that belonged to the service class
cin-mudrā	hand gesture with the index finger touching the thumb indicating Supreme knowledge

Cola-deśa	region ruled by the Colas
darśana	term used for schools of Indian philosophy
dharma	that which sustains; substratum; set of codes and conduct that helps in sustaining and evolving the society; righteousness
graha	one of the nine astronomical bodies that influence life on earth as per our tradition
gṛhastha	householder
gurukula	Vedic schools where the students lived with the teacher for the entire period of education (typically twelve years)
guru–śiṣya	teacher and disciple
haṭhayoga	branch of yoga that deals with regulation of the physical body
iṣṭa-devatā	one's favourite deity
Itihāsa	literally means 'it thus happened'; refers to epics such as the Rāmāyaṇa and Mahābhārata
Jagadguru	literally 'world teacher'; term used to refer to the Śaṅkarācāryas of the Āmnāya-maṭhas
jīvanmukta	the one who is liberated while in the body
jñāna-kāṇḍa	section of the Vedas dealing with philosophy and knowledge of the

	Supreme; comprises the āraṇyaka and Upaniṣad portions
jñānī	a realised person
karma	ritualistic action; destiny that is generated by the actions of the past
karma-kāṇḍa	ritualistic section of the Vedas comprising the saṁhitā and Brāhmaṇam portions
Kirāta	refers to Śiva in the form of a hunter
kṣetra	place of spiritual importance
kśetra-māhātmya	text describing the legends, stories and history surrounding the origin and greatness of places of spiritual importance, especially temples, the modes of worship, the rites and rituals followed, the benefits of visiting the temple, and the devotees of the deity/ies in the temple
kumbhaka	retention of breath
liṅga	mark or symbol; typically used in the context of Śiva-liṅga, which means the mark or symbol of Śiva or Brahman in the form of an ellipsoid, indicating no beginning or end for Brahman
mahātmā	a great soul revered by others
mantra	verses of the Vedas; mystical sounds accompanied by specific intonations that are revealed to the Vedic seers
maṭha	monastic institution

mumukṣutva	intense desire for liberation
Nāga	serpent gods
nirvāṇa	liberation as per Buddhism; merging into nothingness
nirvikalpa-samādhi	permanent absorption into the Self
nivedya	offering to the Lord
padmāsana	cross-legged seating posture
paṇḍita	scholar
paramparā	lineage or tradition
Paraśurāma	considered the sixth incarnation of Lord Viṣṇu, son of Sage Jamadagni and Reṇukā, he is said to have vanquished the Kṣatriya race twenty-one times
pūjā-vidhāna	method of worship
Purāṇa	texts that speak of creation, dissolution, genealogy of Gods and celestials, the reign of various Manus and lineage of kings and dynasties; major Purāṇas are eighteen in number
Ṛṣi	seer of Vedic mantras
rudrākṣa	literally 'the eyes of Śiva', said to have grown from the tears of Śiva; specific type of fruit, the dried form of which is worn (as garlands) by devotees of Śiva
Śaiva	follower of Śiva, and of the theistic tradition of Śiva
Śākta	follower of Śaktī, and the theistic tradition of Śaktī

Śāktī-pīṭha	seat of Śaktī, believed to be fifty-one in number across different parts of Bhārata
sālagrāma	stone obtained from the riverbed of Gandaki; considered as the eternal abode of Lord Viṣṇu
samādhi	absorption into the Self
saṁnyāsa	renunciation
saṁnyāsī	renunciate
sampradāya	lineage or tradition
saṁsāra	the trans-migratory world that comprises birth and death
saṅkalpa	resolution
Śaṅkara-vijaya	biographies of Śaṅkara
śaṅkha	conch – one of the weapons of Lord Viṣṇu
Śāstā	protector deity more commonly found in the southern part of the country; one of the various forms of Śāstā is Dharma-śāstā, who is the deity in the temple at Sabarimala
śāstra	name given to any science in Bhārata, since it directs in a systematic and structured way
Satī	wife of Śiva and daughter of Dakṣa; unable to bear the insult of Śiva, she committed self-immolation
Saura	follower of Sūrya, and of the theistic tradition of Sūrya

siddhānta	principle or doctrine
Swamiyar	ascetic; respectful term used for the ascetics of the monastic institutions of Śaṅkara in Kerala
Tantra	mode of worship that uses aspects (especially physical) beyond the mantras. Sāttvic Tantra uses hand gestures called mudras during worship, while tāmasic Tantra uses various other aspects such as meat, wine, fish and sexual contact.
tīkā	a particular type of commentary
tripuṇḍra	application of three horizontal lines of sacred ash on various parts of the body
upadeśa	instruction
upanayana	investing of the sacred thread and initiation into the 'gāyatrī' mantra
Vaidika	follower of the Vedic tradition
Vaiṣṇava	follower of Viṣṇu, and of the theistic tradition of Viṣṇu
vāmācāra	tāmasic Tāntric approach that uses madya (alcohol), māṁsa (meat), matysa (fish), maithuna (sexual contact), and mudra (gestures) in its rituals in addition to many occult practices
varada-mudra	hand gesture suggesting grant of all wishes

Varāha	considered the third incarnation of Viṣṇu who protected the Earth from annihilation
Vedānta	essence, culmination or summit of the Vedas; Upaniṣads
vigraha	form of the deity, typically made of stone, wood, metal, or other materials; something that conveys specific aspects/features of the deity
Vyāsa	the sage who is credited with classifying of the Vedas, and composition of the *Brahmasūtras*, Mahābhārata and the eighteen Purāṇas
yati	ascetic
yogī	adept in yoga

APPENDIX 7

FAQs

1. *Śaṅkara seems to be attributed with many things – Vedānta, Tantra, mantra, etc. How is it possible that one individual could be an expert in so many things? Was it done by different people and attributed to* Śaṅkara*?*

   Have we not seen prodigies with multiple talents, excelling in each of the fields, even today? Śaṅkara was indeed a prodigy, with excellent grasping power. Being born into a Nambūdiri community in Kerala, he was also naturally advantaged to grow up in an environment that was vibrant with Vedic studies, mantras and tantras. Hence, it is no surprise that Śaṅkara was an adept in multiple śāstras. Attribution of works to a more popular personality, desirous of the work becoming well known is an oft-observed phenomenon. Scholars, hence, look at multiple aspects (e.g., style of writing, usage of words) to ascertain the authenticity of authorship. However, none of this can take away the greatness of the works of Śaṅkara.

2. *Śaṅkara is said to have accomplished so much, and toured the entire Bhārata, at least two times by foot – all in a span of 24 years! Is this all humanly possible?*

The greatest validation of this is the Mahaswami of Kanchi (His Holiness Śrī Chandrashekarendra Saraswati), a mahātmā who lived in the last century. He, after the age of eighty, undertook a country-wide pāda-yātrā, covering a few kilometres every day. He would stay overnight in a village on the way, perform ablutions in the morning and start off to travel to another village. In this way, he ended up travelling several thousand kilometres in a span of few years. We must also bear in mind that Śaṅkara was a great yogī. *Yoga-sūtras* of Patañjali speak of power of great yogis to be able to also travel by air.[1]

3. *There's a popular story of* Śaṅkara *getting into the body of a king to acquire the knowledge of sex. Is that a true story and what is the context?*

This story appears in the MSV and many other biographies of the Ācārya. The context given is that of Ubhaya-bhāratī, the wife of Maṇḍana Miśra, questioning Śaṅkara on the Kāma-śāstra. Śaṅkara, being a saṁnyāsī who came directly from brahmacarya, is said to have admitted ignorance of this topic. Hence he entered the dead body of a king (identified as Amaruka or Amarasiṁha), lived his life through the body of the king to understand the experience of Kāma-śāstra, and then came back as Śaṅkara to respond to Ubhaya-bhāratī. The poems that Amaruka composed during this period are believed to be the Amaru-śataka. The author, however, finds a fundamental dissonance in this story. For a mahātmā who is a great yogī and a

Brahma-jñānī, we understand from the śāstras that everything becomes known. And under 'everything' comes Kāma-śāstra as well. He becomes omniscient, omnipresent and omnipotent just like Īśvara. Also, why would a great scholar of the repute of Ubhaya-bhāratī, who was herself a master of mīmāṁsā and Vedānta, resort to debate on such matters when the discussions between Śaṅkara and Maṇḍana were at a completely different level?

4. *There is also a story of* Śaṅkara *being affected by black magic and subjected to physical pain because of that. Is that true? Do realised souls also have pain and suffering?*

The Śaṅkara-vijayas do speak of the incident of a practitioner of black magic and occult practices called Navagupta manifesting a kind of fistula in the body of the Ācārya. When many of Ācārya's followers had adopted the path of Advaita-vedānta during his visit to the region of Kāmarūpa (part of modern-day Assam), it triggered this act of vengeance. Though Ācārya is said to have not bothered about this, Padmapāda overcome by devotion to his guru is said to have used the power of mantras to cure the same.

Such incidents can be seen in the lives of mahatmas, such as the manifestation of cancer of the throat in Ramakrishna Paramahamsa or sarcoma in Ramana Maharshi. Ācārya, Ramakrishna Paramahamsa, Maharshi and other realised beings like them are constantly revelling in the bliss of the Self inside. For them, the physical world, the physical body within it and the vagaries of the physical body (including ailments) are but temporary appearances like that of a water bubble! In such a state, why will they care even an iota for a physical ailment? Hence, though their body would be subjected to pain like any other human body, they do not suffer the pain.

5. *Śaṅkara is said to have put an end to the seventy-two odd faiths that existed in Bhārata and established only six of them as legitimate. Is that true? If yes, isn't that destroying the diversity of faiths and exhibiting intolerance towards other faiths?*

   Any faith is acceptable so long as it does not infringe on another's well-being and belief systems. Some of the faiths that Śaṅkara encountered (see 'Adhyāya #15: Śaṅkara and the various traditions') were dangerous to the society and its well-being. These are the faiths that Śaṅkara opposed. It may be noted here that, in almost all cases, Śaṅkara engaged in intellectual debates and won over the leaders of these faiths by the sharpness and brilliance of his logic and arguments, not by violence or other ugly forms of power such as mass conversions that are being resorted to by some faiths today. The leaders, transformed by Ācārya's arguments, abandoned their faiths and embraced Vedic dharma. Hence, it would not be fair to accuse Ācārya of destroying any faith. It would be more apt to state that the faiths could not stand the test of Ācārya's arguments and could not hold back their followers from adopting Vedic dharma.

6. *If* Śaṅkara *was a realised soul, why did he engage in so many worldly activities such as writing, speaking, arguing, and travelling? Could he not have just remained silent?*
All realised souls, though alike internally, in their realisation of the Self, vary externally as per their destiny, laws of nature and need of the hour. Janaka, though a realised being (as inferred from the Upaniṣads), lived the life of a king and successfully discharged his duties. The Mahābhārata speaks of a butcher called Dharma-vyādha who was a realised being, but was a gṛhastha, taking care of his family and carrying out his occupation of selling meat. Lord Rāma and Lord Kṛṣṇa, though realised beings (as inferred from the *Yoga-vāsiṣṭa* and *Bhagavad Gītā*), lived the life of a king and cowherd/king, respectively! Hence, we cannot compare realised beings externally. Śaṅkara came at a time when it was essential to travel, speak, write and argue intellectually to get the dharma back on track. Beyond being a realised soul, he was a kāraṇa-puruṣa (one with a bigger purpose) as well.

7. *Advaita-vedānta, as per* Śaṅkara, *is 'Brahman is real, world is illusory, and I am Brahman'. However, no one seems to experience this in practice. Isn't this an imaginary philosophy?*
First, Advaita-vedānta is not as per Śaṅkara. It is as per the Upaniṣads, which Śaṅkara merely transmitted to us. Śaṅkara speaks of three levels of truth (1) vyāvahārika-sattā, i.e., truth of the phenomenal world related to our

body, mind and intellect[2] (2) prātibhāsika-sattā, i.e., the illusory world perceived with the phenomenal world as substratum[3] and (3) pāramārthika-sattā, i.e., the highest truth which is Brahman.[4] Śaṅkara does not negate (1) and (2). He just states that it is temporary and hence not eternal. The only eternal truth is (3). (1) and (2) are already known to us by our own body, mind and intellect. Hence Vedānta and Śaṅkara have no interest or intent in explaining (1) and (2). Their focus is to give us the knowledge of (3), which is not known naturally, and hence we need the śāstras (Vedānta) to inform us of the same. Thus, the dictum 'Brahman is real, world is illusory, and I am Brahman' is the truth as seen from (3) and not from (1) and (2).

As an example, when we experience various events in our dreams, for us, in those moments of dream, they are real experiences. Are they not? As real as the waking state experiences, isn't it? However, when we wake up, we realise the dream experiences to be unreal. They are unreal, not because they were not experienced, but because they no more exist in the waking state.

Even in our waking state, if we observe things from a distance, we realise the short life span everything around us has. The person we see today disappears tomorrow, just like the disappearance of a bubble. Thus, on seeing everything as short-lived, the question of what is permanent arises. That is the quest of Vedānta that ultimately arrives at the answer that 'Life' itself is permanent, in which things appear and disappear. This is called Brahman. Hence the dictum 'Brahman is real, world is illusory, and I am Brahman'.

8. *Are all the biographies on* Śaṅkara *unanimous on his life and times?*

   The simple answer is 'No'. Nearly all the biographies (see 'List of works on Śaṅkara') have been written centuries after Śaṅkara's time. They differ with each other on various aspects, such as place of birth, parents, disciples, temples visited, Maṭhas established, place and time of disappearance, etc. Hence, just based on their unanimity, nothing much can be established. This is what adds the most complexity in ascertaining, with confidence, many aspects in the life of the Ācārya. The most popular version of Śaṅkara's life that is known today is mostly based on the *Madhavīya-śaṅkara-vijaya* of Vidyāraṇya.

9. *Why is there so much of confusion and ambiguity regarding the date of* Śaṅkara?

   Our Ṛṣis have never felt it important to speak of themselves. What mattered to them is the content of what is being said. This has been the tradition of Sanātana-dharma. Hence, we always find it difficult to know the personal details of our great Ṛṣis who have contributed so much to our dharma – be it our Vedic Ṛṣis, Vālmīki, Vyāsa or Śaṅkara.

   Today, dating of our Ṛṣis is becoming a necessity, because our literature and Ṛṣis are being viewed from the lens of Western understanding of history, literature and research. Added to this is the challenge of many scholars deliberately wanting to push Indic personalities and Indic works to as later a time period as possible (preferably CE), so that the antiquity and indigenous wisdom of Bhārata can be attributed to influence from and aping of the West. This began with the works such as 'dating the Vedas' by Western scholars. All these have resulted in ambiguity and confusion on the date of Śaṅkara as well. The topic has been dealt in a very concise way under the section 'Date of Śaṅkara: A brief note'.

Notes

Adhyāya 1: Prelude

1 धरति लोकान् इति धर्मः (*Amarakośa* 3.3.139).

2 वेदोऽखिल धर्ममूलम् (*Manusmṛti* 2.6).

3 द्विविधो हि वेदोक्तो धर्मः प्रवृत्तिलक्षणो निवृत्तिलक्षणश्च (Bhagavad Gītā *Śaṅkara-bhāṣya* Introduction).

4 यदा यदा हि धर्मस्य ग्लानिर्भवति भारत | अभ्युत्थानमधर्मस्य तदात्मानं सृजाम्यहम् (Bhagavad Gītā 4.7).

5 Another example of this is 'Asura' (meaning one who gives life) in Vedic literature – this refers to Varuṇa, which became 'Ahura' in the Persian culture.

Adhyāya 2: The Divine Descent

1 *Thus Spake the Divine* vol. 5, pp. 624–625.

2 *Sōttha nambi enṛu toṇḍar miṇḍittoḍarndu azhaikkum* (*Periya tirumozhi* 2.2.6).

3 *Sankaracharya*, p. 12

4 अद्यापि तद्देशे तज्जातीय द्रविडेशु तैत्तिरीयशाखाया एव प्राचुर्योपलब्धेः (*MSV* ṭīkā 2.6).

5 Among the Upaniṣad Bhāṣyas of Ācārya, we find that he has begun with an invocation and an introduction, as if beginning a new work, only for three Upaniṣads – Bṛhadāraṇyaka, Taittirīya and Māṇḍūkya. Of these, the introduction of the Taittirīya is special. It begins with three verses of invocation and is then followed by a long generic introduction explaining the definition and purpose of the Upaniṣads, which would be apt for the beginning of any major work. Hence many believe this should have been the first Upaniṣad the Ācārya commented on followed closely by the Bṛhadāraṇyaka (belonging to *Śukla Yajurveda*), which also has a small introduction.

6 The Complete Works of Swami Vivekananda/ Volume 8/ Lectures and Discourses/ Women Of India

7 ततो महेशः किल केरलेषु श्रोमद्वृषाद्रौ करुणासमुद्रः । पूर्णानदीपुण्यतटे स्वयम्भूलिङ्गात्मनाऽनङ्गध गाविरासीत् || (MSV 2.1).

8 शं करोतीति शङ्करः (*Amarakośa* 1.1.25).

9 The texts that speak elaborately on these saṁskāras and many other things are called the Gṛhya-sūtras.

10 मधुमासे सिते पक्षे उच्चस्थे ग्रहपञ्चके नक्षत्रे रुद्रदेवत्ये रुद्रांशत्वावबोधके | पूर्णात्मज्ञानपिशुने पूर्णाख्ये पञ्चमीतिथौ (BA 1.59).

Adhyāya 3: The Making of the Mumukṣu

1 यथा मातृमान्पितृमानाचार्यवान्ब्रूयात् (*Bṛhadāraṇyaka-upaniṣad* 4.1.2); माता यस्य विद्यते पुत्रस्य सम्यगनुशास्त्री अनुशासनकर्त्री स मातृमान् explains Śaṅkara in his bhāṣya.

2 The eighteen branches of knowledge included the four Vedas (*Ṛgveda, Yajurveda, Sāmaveda, Atharvaveda*), the six Vedāngas or limbs of Vedas (Śikṣā, Kalpa, Nirukta, Vyākaraṇa, Chandas, Jyotiṣa), the four upa-Vedas or auxiliary sciences (Dhanurveda, Sthāpatya-veda, Gāndharva-veda and Āyurveda), Purāṇas, Mīmāṁsā, Nyāya, and Dharmaśāstras.

3 श्रिया देयम् । ह्रिया देयम् । भिया देयम् । संविदा देयम् (*Taittirīya-upaniṣad Śīkṣāvalli* 11.3).

4 अनन्याश्चिन्तयन्तो मां ये जनाः पर्युपासते । तेषां नित्याभियुक्तानां योगक्षेमं वहाम्यहम् (Bhagavad Gītā 9.22)

Adhyāya 4: The Union of Guru and Śiṣya

1 अहिंसा प्रतिष्ठायां तत्सन्निधौ वैरत्यागः (*Pātañjala-yoga-sūtra* 2.35).

2 न भूमिर्न तोयं न तेजो न वायुः न खं नेन्द्रियं वा न तेषां समूहः । अनेकान्तिकत्वात् सुषुप्त्येकसिद्धः तदेकोऽवशिष्टः शिवः केवलोऽहम् (*Daśaślokī* verse 1).

3 प्रसादेन गुरोः सेयं प्रवृद्धा सूयते फलम् (*Viveka-cūḍāmaṇi* verse 28).

4 सर्ववेदान्तसिद्धान्तगोचरं तमगोचरम् । गोविन्दं परमानन्दं मद्गुरुं प्रणतोऽस्म्यहम् (*Viveka-cūḍāmaṅi* verse 1).

Adhyāya 6: Towards Deva-bhūmi

1 तत्राग्निमाधाय समित्समिद्धय तमेवमूर्त्यन्तरमष्टमूर्तिः स्वयं विधाता तपसः फलानां केनापि कामेन तपश्चचार (*Kumārasambhavam* 1.57).

2 Pouring of water, sanctified by Vedic mantras, from nine pots.

3 Preparation made of rice, milk and sugar.

Adhyāya 7: Establishing the Core of Advaita-vedānta

1 तदर्थाविष्करणायानेकैर्विवृतपदपदार्थवाक्यार्थन्यायमपि अत्यन्तविरुद्धानेकार्थवत्वेन लौकिकैर्गृह्यमाणमुपलभ्य अहं विवेकतोऽर्थनिर्धारणार्थं सङ्क्षेपतो विवरणं करिष्यामि (Bhagavad Gītā *Śaṅkara-bhāṣya* Introduction).

2 Three Prasthānas or pathways – Śruti prasthāna, i.e., pathway of the Vedas (Upaniṣads), Smṛti prasthāna, i.e., pathway of the Smṛtis (Bhagavad Gītā) and Nyāya prasthāna, i.e., pathway of logic (*Brahmasūtra*).

3 शिष्यते अननेति शासनं शास्त्रम् (*Amarakośa* 3.3.179).

4 अल्पाक्षरं असन्दिग्धं सारवत् विश्वतोमुखम् अस्तोभं अनवद्यं च सूत्रं सूत्रविदो विदुः (Traditional verse).

5 सूत्रार्थो वर्ण्यते यत्र वाक्यैः सूत्रानुसारिभिः स्वपदानि च वर्ण्यन्ते भाष्यं भाष्यविदो विदुः (Traditional vesre).

6 देवात्मशक्तिं स्वगुणैर्निगूढाम् (*Śvetāśvatara-upaniṣad* 1.3).

7 याश्च माया मायिनां विश्वमिन्व त्वे पूर्वीः संदधुः पृष्टबन्धो (*Ṛgveda* 3.20.3).

8 मही मित्रस्य वरुणस्य माया चन्द्रेव भानुं वि दधे पुरुत्रा (Ibid. 3.61.7).

9 इन्द्रो मायाभिः पुरुरूप ईयते युक्ता ह्यस्य हरयः शता दशेति (*Bṛhadāraṇyaka-upaniṣad* 2.5.19).

10 मायां तु प्रकृतिं विद्यान्मायिनं च महेश्वरम् (*Śvetāśvatara-upaniṣad* 4.10).

11 दैवी ह्येषा गुणमयी मम माया दुरत्यया । मामेव ये प्रपद्यन्ते मायामेतां तरन्ति ते (Bhagavad Gītā 7.14).

Adhyāya 8: The Approval of Vyāsa

1 तदन्तरप्रतिपत्तौ रंहति सम्परिष्वक्तः प्रश्ननिरूपणाभ्याम् – 'to obtain another body (the soul) goes enveloped (by subtle elements) (as appears from) the question and explanation' (*Brahmā-sūtra* 3.1.1 with English translation by V. Panoli).

2 The term mīmāṁsā means critical analyses. Mīmāṁsā-śāstra focuses on the critical analysis of the Vedas. The part that focuses on the 'Karma-kāṇḍa' section of the Vedas is called pūrva-mīmāṁsā (or simply mīmāṁsā), and that which focuses on the 'Jñāna- kāṇḍa' section of the Vedas is called uttara-mīmāṁsā (or Vedānta). In modern terminology, mīmāṁsā-śāstra deals with the science of hermeneutics. Traditionally, study of three śāstras was considered mandatory for the proper understanding of any subject – science of grammar (Vyākaraṇa also called pada-śāstra), science of interpretation or hermeneutics (mīmāṁsā also called vākya-śāstra) and science of epistemology (Nyāya also called pramāṇa śāstra). One who studied these was called a pada-vākya-pramāṇa-jña.

Adhyāya 9: The Debate with Maṇḍana

1 मुरारिकायकालिमाललामवारिधारिणी (*Yamunāṣṭakam* verse 1).

2 सोऽन्तकाले प्राप्ते सत्यात्मानमात्मनः प्राप्तिद्वारं याचते "हिरण्मयेन पात्रेण सत्यस्यापिहितं मुखम्... अग्ने नय सुपथा राये..." (*Īśāvāsya-upaniṣad Śaṅkara-bhāṣya* 15–18).

3 आम्नायस्य क्रियार्थत्वादानर्थक्यमतदर्थानां तस्मादनित्यमुच्यते (*Mīmāṁsā-sūtra* of Jaimini 1.2.1).

4 चित्तस्य शुद्धये कर्म न वस्तूपलब्धये वस्तुसिद्धिर्विचारेण न किञ्चित् कर्मकोटिभिः (*Viveka-cūḍāmaṅi* verse 11).

Adhyāya 10: To the Sacred Mount of Śiva

1 वरं त्विष्टिकायां समन्यस्तपादं | प्रमाणं भवाब्धेरिदं मामकानां नितम्बः कराभ्यां धृतो येन तस्मात् । (*Pāṇḍuraṅgāṣṭakam* verses 2–3).

2 सह्याद्रिशीर्षे विमले वसन्तं गोदावरितीरपवित्रदेशे । यद्दर्शनात् पातकं पाशु नाशं प्रयाति तं त्र्यम्बकमीशमीडे (*Dvādaśa-jyotirliṅga-stotra* verse 10).

3 यं डाकिनिशाकिनिकासमाजे निषेव्यमाणं पिशिताशनैश्च । सदैव भीमादिपदप्रसिद्धं तं शङ्करं भक्तहितं नमामि (Ibid. verse 6).

4 इलापुरे रम्यविशालकेऽस्मिन् समुल्लसन्तं च जगद्वरेण्यम् । वन्दे महोदारतरस्वभावं घृष्णेश्वराख्यं शरणं प्रपद्ये (Ibid. verse 12).

5 याम्ये सदङ्गे नगरेतिरम्ये विभूषिताङ्गं विविधैश्च भोगैः । सद्भक्तिमुक्तिप्रदमीशमेकं श्रीनागनाथं शरणं प्रपद्ये (Ibid. verse 8).

6 पूर्वोत्तरे प्रज्वलिकानिधाने सदा वसं तं गिरिजासमेतम् । सुरासुराराधितपादपद्मं श्रीवैद्यनाथं तमहं नमामि (Ibid. verse 5).

7 सिद्धिं तथाविधमनोविलयां समाधौ | श्री शैलशृङ्ग कुहरेषु कदोपलप्स्ये (*Yoga-tārāvalī* verse 28).

8 राजीवे भ्रमराधिपो विहरतां श्री शैलवासी विभु (*Śivānandalaharī* verse 51).

9 सेवे श्रीगिरि मल्लिकार्जुनं महालिङ्गं शिवालिङ्गितम् (Ibid. verse 50).

Adhyāya 11: Arrival of the 'Realised Śiṣya'

1 स्वर्णरेखाङ्कितं लिङ्गं नास्ति नास्ति जगत्त्रये वामभागाधिकं लिङ्गं न भूतो न भविष्यति (traditional verse).

2 प्राप्य पुण्यकृतां लोकानुषित्वा शाश्वतीः समाः । शुचीनां श्रीमतां गेहे योगभ्रष्टोऽभिजायते ॥ अथवा योगिनामेव कुले भवति धीमताम् । एतद्धि दुर्लभतरं लोके जन्म यदीदृशम् ॥ तत्र तं बुद्धिसंयोगं लभते पौर्वदेहिकम् । यतते च ततो भूयः संसिद्धौ कुरुनन्दन ॥ पूर्वाभ्यासेन तेनैव ह्रियते ह्यवशोऽपि सः । जिज्ञासुरपि योगस्य शब्दब्रह्मातिवर्तते ॥ प्रयत्नाद्यतमानस्तु योगी संशुद्धकिल्बिषः । अनेकजन्मसंसिद्धस्ततो याति परां गतिम् ॥ (Bhagavad Gītā 6.41–45).

3 कस्त्वं शिशो कस्य कुतोऽसि गन्ता किं नाम ते त्वं कुत आगतोऽसि । एतन्मयोक्तं वद चार्भक त्वं मत्प्रीतये प्रीति विवर्धनोऽसि (*Hastāmalakīyam* verse 1).

4 स नित्योपलब्धिस्वरूपोऽहमात्मा (Refrain of *Hastāmalakīyam*).

Adhyāya 12: In the Land of Ṛṣyaśṛṅga

1 नमस्ते शारदे देवी काश्मीरपुरवस्सिनी | त्वामहं प्रार्थये नित्यं विद्यादानं च देहि मे || (traditional verse).

2 करुणावरुणालय पालय मां (*Toṭakāṣṭaka* verse 2).

3 Sureśvara says that he is composing the *Naiṣkarmya siddhi* by the command of his guru – वक्ष्ये गुर्वनुशिक्षया (*Naiṣkarmya-siddhi* verse 3)

Adhyāya 13: The Dutiful Son

1 नमाम्यभोगिपरिवारसम्पदं निरस्तभूतिमनुमार्धविग्रहम् । अनुग्रमुन्मृदितकाललाञ्छनं विना विनायकमपूर्वशङ्करम् (*Pañcapādikā* 1.3).

2 भव एव भवान् (*Toṭakāṣṭakam* verse 4).

3 पुंगवकेतन (Ibid. verse 7).

4 करुणावरुणालय (Ibid. verse 2).

5 गुरुपुंगव (Ibid. verse 7).

6 विदिताखिलशास्त्रसुधाजलधे महितोपनिषत् कथितार्थनिधे (Ibid. verse 1).

7 भवता जनता सुहिता भविता निजबोधविचारण चारुमते (*Toṭakāṣṭakam* verse 3).

8 गरीयसे नमस्तस्मा अविद्याग्रन्थिभेदिने (*Naiṣkarmya-siddhi* 2).

9 यस्येदं सकलामलेन्दुकिरणप्रख्यैर्यशोरश्मिभिः (*Taittirīya-upaniṣad-bhāṣya-vārtika* 2).

Adhyāya 14: Digvijaya

1 इतीव ब्रुवन्गान्धशैलाधिरूढः (*Subrahmaṇya-bhujaṅgam* verse 6); मुनीन्द्रानुकूले सुगन्धाख्यशैले (Ibid. verse 7).

2 इति व्यञ्जयन्सिन्धुतीरे य आस्ते (Ibid. verse 4).

3 पिशाचाश्च सर्वे भवत्पत्रभूतिं विलोक्य क्षणात्तारकारे द्रवन्ते (Ibid. verse 25).

4 अयोध्या मथुरा माया काशी काञ्ची अवन्तिका पुरी द्वारवती चैव सप्तैते मोक्षदायकाः (traditional verse).

5 रागस्वरूप-पाशाढ्या क्रोधाकाराङ्कुशोज्ज्वला | मनोरूपेक्षु-कोदण्डा पञ्चतन्मात्र-सायका (*Lalitā-sahasranāma* verses 2–3).

6 ध्यायेत्पद्मासनस्थां विकसितवदनां पद्मपत्रायताक्षीं (*Lalitā-sahasranāma dhyāna śloka*).

7 धनुर्बाणान् पाशं सृणिमपि दधाना करतलैः (*Saundaryalaharī* verse 7).

8 अपवार्य स तान्त्रिकानतानीद्भगवत्याः श्रुतिसम्मतां सपर्याम् (MSV 15.5).

9 श्रीचक्रं स्थापयामास कामाक्ष्याः पुरो गुरुः (BA 8.79).

10 प्रकृतिं च गुहाश्रयं महोग्रां स्वकृते चक्रवरे प्रवेश्य योऽग्रे अकृताश्रितसौम्यमूर्तिमार्यां सुकृतं नस्स चिनोतु शङ्करार्यः (*Jagadguru-ratna-mālā-stavam* verse 28).

11 तस्मिन् स्थले मासमात्रं स्थित्वा शङ्कुप्रतिष्ठापूर्वकं शिवकाञ्चीति पट्टणं निर्माय तत्प्राक् ब्रह्मयज्ञकुण्डाविर्भूतविष्णुं वरदराजनामानं समाश्रित्य तत्र विष्णुकाञ्चीति प्रसिद्धं पट्टणं निर्माय तत्सेवार्थं ब्राह्मणादीन् अनेकभक्तजनान् सम्पाद्य तानपि शुद्धाद्वैतवृत्तिन एव कृत्वा सर्ववेदान्ततात्पर्यैकनिष्ठः परमगुरुः सुखमास (PSV ch. 63).

12 पुरुषोत्तमं तु क्षेत्रं स्याज्जगन्नाथो(अ)स्य देवता | विमलाख्या हि देवी स्यादाचार्यः पद्मपादकः (*Maṭhāmnāya* verse 11).

13 काश्मीराख्यं मण्डलं तत्र शस्तं यत्रास्ते असौ शारदा वागधीशा (MSV 16.55).

14 द्वारैर्युक्तं माण्डपैस्तच्चतुर्भिर्दिव्या गेहं यत्र सर्वज्ञपीठम् (Ibid 16.56).

15 काञ्चीनगरे मुक्तिस्थले कदाचिदुपविश्य स्थूलशरीरं सूक्ष्मे अन्तर्धाय...सर्वजगद्व्यापकं चैतन्यमभवत् (PSV ch. 74).

Adhyāya 15: Śaṅkara and the Various Traditions

1 गर्भं दधार शिवगर्भमसौ मृगाक्षी (MSV 2.57).

2 भव एव भवान् (*Toṭakāṣṭakam* verse 4); नमाम्यभोगिपरिवारसम्पदं निरस्तभूतिमनुमार्धविग्रहम् । अनुग्रमुन्मृदितकाललाञ्छनं विना विनायकमपूर्वशङ्करम् (*Pañcapādikā* 1.3).

3 मुक्त्वा मौनं वटविटपिनोः मूलतो निष्पतन्ति शम्भोर्मूर्तिः चरति भुवने शङ्कराचार्यरूपा (MSV 4.60).

4 नमः शङ्कराय च मयस्कराय च नमः शिवाय च शिवतराय (*Rudra-praśna* 8th anuvāka).

5 विष्णोरर्धं महाभागं पुत्रमैक्ष्वाकुनंदनम् (Vālmīki-rāmāyaṇa 1.18.11).

6 निशीथे तमौद्भूते जायमाने जनार्दने देवक्यां देवरूपिण्यां विष्णुः सर्वगुहाशयः (*Śrīmad-bhāgavata* 10.3.8).

7 प्रोद्धृत्य कृष्णमचलं शनकैर्भुजाभ्याम् | प्रातिष्ठिपन्निकट एव न यत्र बाधा नद्येत्युदीर्य सुखमास्स्व चिराय चेति | (MSV 3.79).

8 अथवा जीवपुर एवास्मिन् ब्रह्म सन्निहितमुपलक्ष्यते, यथा सालग्रामे विष्णुः सन्निहित इति, तद्वत् (*Brahma-sūtra Śaṅkara-bhāṣya* 1.3.14).

9 नामोपास्स्व ब्रह्मेति ब्रह्मबुद्ध्या — यथा प्रतिमां विष्णुबुद्ध्या उपास्ते, तद्वत् (*Chāndogya-upaniṣad* 7.1.4).

10 यथा विष्ण्वङ्गाङ्कितायां शिलादिप्रतिमायां विष्णुं लोकः, एवम् (*Bṛhadāraṇyaka-upaniṣad* 5.1.1).

11 स आदिकर्ता नारायणाख्यो विष्णुः भौमस्य ब्रह्मणो ब्राह्मणत्वस्य रक्षणार्थं देवक्यां वसुदेवादंशेन कृष्णः किल सम्बभूव (Bhagavad Gītā *Śaṅkara-bhāṣya* introduction).

12 अन्तकाले मरणकाले च मामेव परमेश्वरं विष्णुं स्मरन् मुक्त्वा परित्यज्य कलेबरं शरीरं यः प्रयाति गच्छति, सः मद्भावं वैष्णवं तत्त्वं याति (Bhagavad Gītā 8.5).

13 सच्चिदानन्दरूपाय कृष्णायाक्लिष्टकारिणे नमो वेदान्तवेद्याय गुरवे बुद्धिसाक्षिणे (*Viṣṇu-sahasranāma Śaṅkara-bhāṣya* introduction).

14 श्रियाऽऽश्लिष्टो विष्णुः स्थिरचरगुरुर्वेदविषयो धियां साक्षी शुद्धो हरिरसुरहन्ताब्जनयनः । गदी शङ्खी चक्री विमलवनमाली स्थिररुचिः शरण्यो लोकेशो मम भवतु कृष्णोऽक्षिविषयः (*Kṛṣṇāṣṭakam* verse 1).

15 श्रीमन्नगर-नायिका (*Lalitā-sahasranāma* verse 22).

16 चतुर्भिः श्रीकण्ठैः शिवयुवतिभिः पञ्चभिरपि प्रभिन्नाभिः शम्भोर्नवभिरपि मूलप्रकृतिभिः । चतुश्चत्वारिंशद्वसुदलकलाश्रत्रिवलय त्रिरेखाभिः सार्धं तव शरणकोणाः परिणताः (*Saundaryalaharī* verse 11).

17 सुधासिन्धोर्मध्ये सुरविटपिवाटीपरिवृते मणिद्वीपे नीपोपवनवति चिन्तामणिगृहे । शिवाकारे मञ्चे परमशिवपर्यङ्कनिलयां भजन्ति त्वां धन्याः कतिचन चिदानन्दलहरीम् (*Saundaryalaharī* verse 8).

18 सुधासागर-मध्यस्था (*Lalitā-sahasranāma* verse 23).

19 कदम्बवन-वासिनी (Ibid. verse 23).

20 चिन्तामणि-गृहान्तस्था (Ibid. verse 22).

21 कौल-मार्ग-तत्पर-सेविता (Ibid. verse 93).

22 अकुला समयान्तस्था समयाचार-तत्परा (Ibid. verse 37).

23 द्विसप्ततिमतोच्छेत्ता सर्वदिग्विजयप्रभुः – one who did Digvijaya and uprooted the seventy-two faiths – a name of Ācārya in the श्री-शङ्कराचार्याष्टोत्तरशतनाम-स्तोत्रम्|

24 शिवतत्परसूत्रभाष्यकर्ता प्रहसन् वाचमुवाच शैववर्यः (MSV 15.35).

25 माहेश्वराश्चत्वारः शैवाः, पाशुपताः, कारुणिकसिद्धान्तिनः, कापालिकाश्चेति । चत्वारोऽप्यमी महेश्वरप्रणीतसिद्धान्तानुयायितया माहेश्वराः । कारणमीश्वरः । कार्यं प्राधानिकं महदादि । योगोऽप्योङ्कारादिध्यानधारणादिः । विधिस्त्रिषवणस्नानादिर्गूढचर्यावसानः, दुःखान्तो मोक्षः । पशव आत्मानस्तेषां पाशो बन्धनं तद्विमोक्षो दुःखान्तः । (*Bhāmatī* 2.2.37).

26 माहेश्वरास्तु मन्यन्ते — कार्यकारणयोगविधिदुःखान्ताः पञ्च पदार्थाः पशुपतिनेश्वरेण पशुपाशविमोक्षणायोपदिष्टाः; पशुपतिरीश्वरो निमित्तकारणमिति (*Brahma-sūtra Śaṅkara-bhāṣya* 2.2.37).

27 आक्षिप्य पाशुपतवैष्णववीरशैवमाहेश्वराश्च विजिता हि सुरेश्वराद्यैः (MSV 10.115).

28 ॐ अग्निर्वै देवानामवमो विष्णुः परमः (*Aitareya-brāhmaṇa* 1.1).

29 अष्टाक्षरमन्त्रोपासकाः रक्तचन्दनपुष्पमालाधारिणः षड्विधा भक्ता वर्तन्ते (PSV Ch.13).

30 Earth (or Bhu-loka), six worlds above the earth, i.e., Bhuva, Suva, Maha, Jana, Tapa and Satyam, seven worlds below the earth, i.e., atala, vitala, sutala, rasātala, talātala, mahātala and pātala.

31 प्रतिपद्य तु बाह्लिकान् ... केचिदथा अर्हताभिधाने | (MSV 15.142).

Adhyāya 16: Śaṅkara and Yoga

1 योगश्चित्तवृत्तिनिरोधः (*Pātañjala-yoga-sūtra* 1.2).

2 तदा द्रष्टुः स्वरूपेऽवस्थानम् (Ibid. 1.3).

3 एतेन साङ्ख्यस्मृतिप्रत्याख्यानेन, योगस्मृतिरपि प्रत्याख्याता द्रष्टव्येत्यतिदिशति (*Brahma-sūtra Śaṅkara-bhāṣya* 2.1.3).

4 अतः सम्प्रतिपन्नार्थैकदेशत्वादष्टकादिस्मृतिवद्योगस्मृतिरप्यनपवदनीया भविष्यतीति (Ibid. 2.1.3).

5 योगशास्त्रप्रसिद्धा मनसः पञ्च वृत्तयः परिगृह्यन्ते 'प्रमाणविपर्ययविकल्पनिद्रास्मृतयः' (पा. यो. सू. १ । १ । ६) नाम (*Brahma-sūtra Śaṅkara-bhāṣya* 2.4.12).

6 एषैव च योगशास्त्रेषु योगिनामनेकशरीरयोगप्रक्रिया (Ibid. 4.4.15).

7 अत एव पद्मकादीनामासनविशेषाणामुपदेशो योगशास्त्रे (Ibid. 4.1.10).

8 हृदयादूर्ध्वं प्रवृत्ता सुषुम्ना नाम नाडी योगशास्त्रेषु प्रसिद्धा (*Taittirīya-upaniṣad Śaṅkara-bhāṣya* 1.6.2).

9 ज्ञानेन्द्रियाणि सर्वाणि निरुध्य मनसा सह | एकत्वभावना योगः क्षेत्रज्ञपरमात्मनोः || (*Viṣṇu-sahasranāma Śaṅkara-bhāṣya* 16).

10 सहस्रशः सन्तु हठेषु कुम्भाः सम्भाव्यते केवलकुम्भ एव (*Yoga-tārāvali* verse 10).

11 सदाशिवोक्तानि सपादलक्षलयावधानानि वसन्ति लोके । नादानुसन्धानसमाधिमेकं मन्यामहे मान्यतमं लयानाम् || (Ibid. verse 2).

12 श्री आदिनाथेन सपादकोटिलयप्रकाराः कथिता जयन्ति | नादानुसन्धानकमेकमेव मन्यामहे मुख्यतमं लयानाम् || (*Haṭhayoga-pradīpikā* verse 4.66).

13 उन्मन्यवाप्यते शीघ्रं भ्रूध्यानं मम संमतम् | राजयोगपदं प्राप्तुं सुखोपयोल्पचेतसाम् | सद्यः प्रत्ययसंधायि जायते नादजो लयः || (*Haṭhayoga-pradīpikā* 4.80).

14 निश्वासलोपैर्निभृतैः शरीरैर्नेत्राम्बुजैरर्धनिमीलितैश्च । आविर्भवन्तीममनस्कमुद्रामालोकयामो मुनिपुङ्गवानाम् || (*Yoga-tārāvali* verse 21).

15 सिद्धिं तथाविधमनोविलयां समाधौ श्रीशैलशृङ्गकुहरेषु कदोपलप्स्ये | (Ibid. verse 28).

Adhyāya 17: Tradition of Śaṅkara

1 ब्रह्मचर्यं परिसमाप्य गृही भवेद्गृही भूत्वा वनी भवेद्वनी भूत्वा प्रव्रजेत् । यदि वेतरथा ब्रह्मचर्यादेव प्रव्रजेद्गृहाद्वा वनाद्वा (*Jābāla-upaniṣad* 4).

2 संन्यासः षड्विधो भवति । कुटीचको बहूदको हंसः परमहंसः तुरीयातीतोऽवधूतश्चेति (*Nārada-parivrājaka-upaniṣad* 5).

3 Also called *Kālikā-maṭha*.

4 Also called *Śrī-maṭha*.

5 BSV states it as Śāradā.

6 मठं च स्थापयामास तत्र विद्याभिवृद्धये (BA 8.79).

7 कामाक्षी तस्य देवी स्यात् सर्वकामफलप्रदा (*Maṭhāmnāya* verse 30).

8 अधिकाञ्चि च शारदामठं योऽभ्यधिकं नस्सुखमातनोतु सोऽयम् (*Jagadguru-ratna-mālā-stava* verse 31).

9 தன்னிலை திகழ்த்தியித்துதியிற்றன் மயஞ்சொன்னவச்சங்க ரன்றுன்னுமென்னுளே (*Dakṣiṇāmūrti-stotram maṅgalācaraṇa*)

10 ब्राह्मणाचारदेवाः स्युरीशो विष्णुर्दिनेश्वरः उमा गणपतिश्चैव तेषां पूजापरा नराः (PSV Ch. 6).

11 Subrahmaṇya is regarded as one born of fire, i.e., agnibhū, or the fire sparks of Śiva.

Appendix 2: Date of Śaṅkara: A Brief Note

1 न मृत्युर्न शङ्का न मे जातिभेदः पिता नैव मे नैव माता न जन्म (*Nirvāṇa ṣaṭkam* verse 5).

Appendix 3 List of Śaṅkara's Works

1 Sequence as per the traditional verse ईश-केन-कठ-प्रश्न-मुण्ड-माण्डुक्य-तित्तिरी | ऐतरेयं-च-छान्दोग्यं-बृहदारण्यकं-दशा ||

Appendix 7: FAQs

1 कायाकाशयोः सम्बन्धसंयमाल्लघुतूल-समापत्तेश्चाकाशगमनम् (*Pātañjala-yoga-sūtra* 3.43).

2 तद्विकारो अनृतेऽपि देहशुङ्गे ब्रह्मोपलभ्यत इति ब्रह्मपुरमित्युक्तं व्यावहारिकम् (*Chāndogya-upaniṣad Śaṅkara-bhāṣya* 8.1.5).

3 तथा च लोकेऽनुभवः — शुक्तिका हि रजतवदवभासते, एकश्चन्द्रः सद्वितीयवदिति (*Brahma-sūtra adhyāsa-bhāṣya*).

4 न तेन परमार्थरूपस्य ब्रह्मणः संस्पर्शः (*Brahma-sūtra Śaṅkara-bhāṣya* 1.2.8).

References

Antarkar, W.R. (1962). *Śaṅkara Vijaya-saṅgraha by Puruṣottama Bhāratī.* Oriental Thought, pp. 1–16.

——— (1965). *Śrī Śaṅkarābhyudaya-mahākāvya by Tirumala Dīkṣita.* Journal of the University of Mumbai, pp. 138–87.

——— (1964). *Śrī Śaṅkarābhyudaya-kāvya by Nīlakaṇṭha.* Journal of the University of Mumbai, pp. 128–67.

——— (1968). आचार्य विजयः by श्रीपरमेश्वर कविकण्ठीरव. *Journal of the University of Mumbai*, pp. 1–69.

——— (1973). श्री चिद्विलासमुनिविरचितः शङ्करविजयविलास. Bhāratīya Vidyā, pp. 1–92.

——— (1992). *Śrī Śaṅkarācārya Caritam of Śrī Govindanātha.* Bhāratīya Vidyā, pp. 57–141.

——— (2003). *Shankara Vijayas: A Comparative and a Critical Study.* Mumbai: Veda Shastra Pandit Raksha Sabha.

Chandrasekharan, T. (1954). *Śaṅkara-vijaya by Vyāsācala.* Madras: Government Press.

Chattopadhyaya, S. (2000). *Evolution of Hindu Sects up to the Time of Shankaracharya.* New Delhi: Munshiram Manoharlal Publishers.

Chinmayananda, S. (1978). *Sankara the Missionary.* Mumbai: Central Chinmaya Mission Trust.

Clarke, M. (2006). *The Daśanāmī Saṁnyāsīs.* Boston: BRILL.

Devasenapathi, V. A. (1975). *Kamakottam Nayanmars and Adi Shankara.* Madras: The Institute of Traditional Cultures.

Gurunatha (1898). श्रीशङ्करविजयचूर्णिका. Mumbai: Nirnaya Sagara Press.

Iyer, A.N., and Sastri, S.L. (1962). *The traditional age of Sri Shankaracharya and the Mutts.* Madras: Thomson & Co. Pvt Ltd.

Iyer, R. K. *The Truth about the Kumbakonam Mutt* - Parts 1 & 2 (1965). Madurai: Sri Ramakrishna Press.

Kuppuswami, A. (2013). *Sri Shankaracharya and His Connection with Kanchipuram*. Mahesh Krishnamoorthy.

Lorenzen, D.N. (1991). *Kapalikas and Kalamukhas: Two Lost Saivite Sects*. Delhi: Motilal Banarsidass.

Mahadevan, T.M. P (1968). *Preceptors of Advaita*. Secunderabad: Sri Kanchi Kamakoti Sankara Mandir.

Mahadevan, T.M.P (1968). *Sankaracharya*. Delhi: National Book Trust.

Mathamnaya from Brhat Shankara Vijaya (Chapter 13). (n.d.). Retrieved from https://archive.org/details/mathamnaya-from-brihat-sankara-vijaya

Mishra, P. (2017). *Shri Jagannath and Adiguru Shankaracharya*. Odisha Review, pp. 35–38.

Mishra, P.N. (2001). *Matamnaya Setu or Mahanushasanam with Sharada Bhashya*. Dwaraka: Shankaracharya Memorial Trust.

Mukhyananda, S. (2006). *Sri Shankaracharya: Life and Philosophy*. Kolkata: Advaita Ashrama.

Namboodiri, P.N. (2013). *Vedāṅgadīpti* (collected works of K.N.M. Divakara Namputiri). Calicut: University of Calicut.

Namboothiri Websites Trust. (n.d.). Retrieved from https://www.namboothiri.com.

Nandakumar, P. (2013). *Adi Sankara: Finite to the Infinite*. Veliyanad: Chinmaya International Foundation.

Nandi, R.N. (1973). *Religious Institutions and Cults in the Deccan* (A.D.. 600–A.D. 1000). Delhi: Motilal Banarsidass.

Nowicka, O. (2019). 'Local Advaita Vedānta Monastic Tradition in Kerala: Locating, Mapping, Networking'. *The Polish Journal of the Arts and Culture*, New Series 9, pp. 27–51.

Panoli, V. (2011). *Prasthanathraya: Brahmasutra*, vol vi. Kozhikode: The Mathrubhumi Printing & Publishing Co. Ltd.

Pardeep, K., and Sangeeta. (2015). *Adi Shankaracharya: The Architect of Pilgrimage Tourism in India*. International Research Journal of Social Sciences, pp. 24–28.

Puninchattaya, V. (n.d). *Edaneer Mutt Edneer*. Shree Gopalakrishna Seva Samstha.

Punya Shloka Manjari (Part 2) of Ram Shastri Mumukshu Bhavan collection. (n.d.). Retrieved from https://archive.org/details/nZUO_punya-shloka-manjari-part-2-of-ram-shastri-mumukshu-bhavan-collection

Ramachandran, V.G. (1985). *Date of Adi Sankara*. Madras: International Society of the Investigation of Ancient Civilizations.

Rao, K.R. (1939). शङ्करजीवनाख्यानम्. Mumbai: Nirnaya Sagara Press.

Rao, T.A. (1986). *Copper Plate Inscriptions Belonging to the Sri Sankaracharya of the Kamakoti Pitha*. Delhi: Gyan Publishing House.

Rukmani, T.S. (1994). *Shankaracharya*. New Delhi: Ministry of Information and Broadcasting, Government of India.

Sanathana, Y., and Hazarika, M. (2019). 'Ancient Pragjyotisha-Kamarupa and Adi Shankaracharya'. *History Today*, pp. 9–15.

Saraswati, H.S. (1980). *Adi Shankara: His Life and Times*. Bombay: Bharatiya Vidya Bhavan.

Saraswati, H.S. (2022). *Thus Spake the Divine* (volume 5). Chennai: Giri Trading Agency.

Saraswati, S.S. (2015). *Śrī Śaṅkara Bhagavatpāda Vṛttānta Ṣāra Sarvasva* (English translation). Holenarasipura: Adhyatma Prakasha Karyalaya.

Sarkar, J. (2022). *A History of Dasanami Naga Sannyasis*. New Delhi: Gyan Publishing House.

Sarkar, S.J. (2023). *A History of Dasnami Naga Sanyasis*. Allahabad: Rashtriya Sahitya Sansthan.

Sastrigal, K.R. (n.d). *Guruvamsakavya by Lakshmana Sastri*. Srirangam: Vani Vilas Press.

Sastry, T.S. (1916). *The Age of Saṅkara*. Madras: B.G. Paul & Co.

Shastri, P.R. (1915). *A Short History of Jagadguru Sri Shankaracharya and His Successors on His Holy Throne*. Sri Rangam: Sri Vani Vilas Press.

Shastri, S.V. (1986). *Sri Shankarabhyudayam by Sri Rajachudamani Dikshit*. Srirangam: Simili Venkatarama Sastri Trust.

Shastri, U. (1981). *The Age of Shankara*. Ghaziabad: Virjanand Vedic Research Institute.

Shastry, D.A. (2009). *The Records of Sringeri Dharmasamsthana*. Sringeri: Sringeri Matha.

Sivadatta (1895). *Pantanjali Charita of Ramabhadra Dikshit*. Bombay: Nirnaya Sagar Press.

Sundareshan, V. (2000). *Conflicting Hagiographies and History: The Place of Shankara Vijaya Texts in Advaita Tradition*. International Journal of Hindu studies, pp. 109–84.

Suri, L. (1927). *Bhagavatpadabhyudayam. Srirangam*: Vani Vilas Press.

Tapasyananda, S. (2002). *Sankara Digvijaya: The traditional Life of Sri Sankaracharya* (Madhava Vidyaranya). Chennai: Sri Ramakrishna Math.

Tarkapanchanana, J. (1868). *Sankara Vijaya by Anandagiri*. Calcutta: Asiatic Society of Bengal.

Unni, N.P. (2006). *Tantra Literature of Kerala*. Delhi: New Bharatiya Book Corporation.

Vaidyanathan, K.R. (1974). *Sri Krishna: The Lord of Guruvayur*. Mumbai: Bharatiya Vidya Bhavan.

Varma, P.K. (2022). *Adi Shankaracharya: Hinduism's Greatest Thinker*. Chennai: Westland Non-Fiction.

Veezhinathan, N. (1971). *Śrī Śaṅkara-vijaya of Anantānandagiri*. Madras: University of Madras.

Venkataraman, N. (2014). *Ātmatīrtham*. Chennai: Rishi Prakasana Sabha Nikaya Trust.

Zoller, C.P. (2017). *Traditions of Transgressive Sacrality (against Blasphemy) in Hinduism*. Acta Orientalia, pp. 1–162.

श्री विद्यारण्यविरचितः श्रीमच्छङ्करदिग्विजयः (Along with Advaita-rājya-lakṣmī Tīkā and Ḍiṇḍimā Vyākhyā of Dhanapati Sūrī). (1891). Pune: Anandashram.

श्री शाङ्करस्तोत्राणि लघुप्रकरणानि च. (2014). *Sringeri*. Dakshinamnaya Sri Sharada Peetham.

Index

About the Author

Subramanian Chidambaran, also known as Subbu, comes from a family of Samavedic scholars in Puthucode village, Palakkad district, Kerala. He graduated in electrical engineering from Veermata Jijabai Technological Institute (VJTI), Mumbai, and holds a postgraduate degree in management from the Indian Institute of Management (IIM), Lucknow. With over fifteen years of experience in management consulting and corporate strategy, he has published several case studies and articles in leading national and international management journals and has delivered lectures at top B-schools in India.

Subbu also holds a master's degree in Sanskrit, specializing in Vedanta, and a diploma in manuscriptology, both from the University of Mumbai, where he has served as a visiting faculty member teaching Vedanta, itihasa, Purāṇas and bhakti. He has formally studied Veda chanting for eight years and is currently pursuing doctoral studies on the topic 'Indic Perspectives for Modern Leadership' at Chinmaya Vishwa Vidyapeeth. He has authored several papers and articles on Indian knowledge systems (IKS), published in various national and international journals, and presented at numerous conferences and seminars.

Coming from a maternal family of music connoisseurs, Subbu began his formal training in Carnatic music at the age of thirteen. He is currently under the tutelage of 'Sangita Kala Acharya' Vidushi Smt. Alamelu Mani, with whom he has been learning for over fifteen years. Subbu has been giving lecture demonstrations and 'Sangeeta Upanyasam' (musical storytelling), combining his interests and skills in music and Indic knowledge. Additionally, he hosts a YouTube channel called *Subbu's Corner*, raising awareness about Sanātana-dharma.